Photo by Richard Anderson
A scene from the Center Stage production of "Miss Evers' Boys." Set design by Douglas Stein.

MISS EVERS' BOYS

BY DAVID FELDSHUH

★

DRAMATISTS
PLAY SERVICE
INC.

For Martha, for everything

ACKNOWLEDGMENT

The playwright wishes to acknowledge the important contribution made to the life and development of MISS EVERS' BOYS by Irene Lewis, director of the play at Center Stage and Mark Taper Forum. He also wishes to acknowledge the contributions of Bonnie Morris and Michael Robins of Illusion Theater, who offered initial and continuing support for the development of the play; and Rick Davis, who served as dramaturg for the Center Stage production.

AUTHOR'S NOTE

This play was suggested by the book, *Bad Blood*, by James H. Jones (The Free Press, 1981) and by a number of primary sources including the Senate testimony, medical articles and field interviews conducted in Alabama in the 1930s. The Tuskegee Study was a grim reality and Professor Jones' book is recommended to all who would desire a meticulously researched, insightful and absorbing review of it.

Although MISS EVERS' BOYS is based on a true event, and although the character of Miss Evers was inspired by a nurse involved in the Tuskegee Study, the play is fiction. The characters (including that of the nurse), the context, and the incidents of the play are products of the playwright's imagination, and any quotations from primary sources have been rearranged, reassigned or paraphrased. MISS EVERS' BOYS is not presented nor intended to be taken as a factual record of real events or real people.

MISS EVERS' BOYS was produced by Center Stage (Stan Wojewodski, Jr., Artistic Director; Peter W. Culman, Managing Director), in Baltimore, Maryland, on November 17, 1989. It was directed by Irene Lewis; the set design was by Douglas Stein; the costume design was by Catherine Zuber; the lighting design was by Pat Collins; the sound design was by Janet Kalas; the music design by Dwight Andrews; the choreography was by Dianne McIntyre and the stage managers were Julie Thompson and Jill Rendall. The cast was as follows:

DR. EUGENE BRODUS	David Downing
WILLIE JOHNSON	K. Todd Freeman
HODMAN BRYAN	Damien Leake
CALEB HUMPHRIES	Delroy Lindo
DR. JOHN DOUGLAS	Ethan Phillips
EUNICE EVERS	Seret Scott
BEN WASHINGTON	Allie Woods, Jr.

MISS EVERS' BOYS was produced by Mark Taper Forum (Gordon Davidson, Artistic Director; Stephen Alpert, Managing Director), in Los Angeles, California, on July 8, 1990, 1990. It was directed by Irene Lewis; the set design was by Douglas Stein; the costume design was by Catherine Zuber; the lighting design was by Pat Collins; the original music was by Olu Dara; the sound design by Jon Gottlieb; the choreography was by Dianne McIntyre; the production stage manager was James T. McDermott and the stage manager was Jill Ragaway. The cast was as follows:

DR. EUGENE BRODUS	Bennet Guillory
WILLIE JOHNSON	K. Todd Freeman
HODMAN BRYAN	Mel Winkler
CALEB HUMPHRIES	Carl Lumbly
DR. JOHN DOUGLAS	Charles Lanyer
EUNICE EVERS	Starletta DuPois
BEN WASHINGTON	John Cothran, Jr.
ATTENDANTS	Hawthorne James, Richardson Morse, Cynthena Sanders, Harry Waters, Jr.

MISS EVERS' BOYS was produced by The Alliance Theatre Company (Kenneth Leon, Artistic Director; Edith H. Love, Managing Director), in Atlanta, Georgia, on September 18, 1990. It was directed by Kenny Leon; the set design was by Michael Olich; the costume design was by Susan E. Mickey; the lighting design was by Robert Peterson; the original music was composed by Dwight Andrews; the dance consultant was Barbara Sullivan and the production stage manager was Pat A. Flora. The cast was as follows:

DR. EUGENE BRODUS .... Chuck Cooper
WILLIE JOHNSON .... Monti Sharp
HODMAN BRYAN .... Donald Griffin
CALEB HUMPHRIES .... Afemo Omilami
DR. JOHN DOUGLAS .... Chris Kayser
EUNICE EVERS .... Carol Mitchell-Leon
BEN WASHINGTON .... Frederick Charles Canada

MISS EVERS' BOYS was produced by The Illusion Theater (Michael Robins, Executive Producing Director; Bonnie Marks, Managing Director), in Minneapolis, Minnesota, on May 3, 1991. It was directed by D. Scott Glassera and Michael Robins; the set design was by Dean Holzman; the costume design was by Katherine Maurer; the lighting design was by Barry Browning; the composer and sound designer was Michael Keck; the choreography was by Marvette Knight and the production stage managers were Robin Macgregor and Chris A. Coe. The cast was as follows:

DR. EUGENE BRODUS .... Brent S. Hendon
WILLIE JOHNSON .... Lester Purry
HODMAN BRYAN .... Mark M. Cryer
CALEB HUMPHRIES .... Dion Graham
DR. JOHN DOUGLAS .... Peter Moore
EUNICE EVERS .... Denise Burse-Mickelbury
BEN WASHINGTON .... T. Mychael Rambo

CHARACTERS

(Note: All the characters except for Dr. Douglas are African-American.)

EUNICE EVERS, 28, a public-health nurse
DR. EUGENE BRODUS, 40, Administrative Head, Memorial Hospital, Tuskegee, Alabama
DR. JOHN DOUGLAS, 34, field physician, United States Public Health Service
WILLIE JOHNSON, 19, a tenant farmer
CALEB HUMPHRIES, 25, a tenant farmer
HODMAN BRYAN, 37, a tenant farmer
BEN WASHINGTON, 57, a tenant farmer

TIME

ACT ONE
1932–Contagion

ACT TWO
1946–Progression
1972–End Point

PLACE

Tuskegee, Alabama

PRODUCTION NOTES

The physical setting for MISS EVERS' BOYS is the Possom Hollow Schoolhouse located in a rural area outside of the town of Tuskegee, in Macon County, Alabama. This type of wooden, white-washed, one-room school was constructed in the South by a New York foundation "dedicated to the education of Negro youth." The interior of the school reveals two benches and a table, a cracked blackboard, and a rope to an exterior bell. In the open space in front of and around the school, other suggested and emblematic settings present themselves. Finally, there are changing "testimony areas," closely defined by light and meant suggest testimony offered inside the schoolhouse to members of a Senate subcommittee investigating human experimentation in general and the Tuskegee study in particular in 1972.

The theatrical setting of MISS EVERS' BOYS is the conscience and memory of Eunice Evers and it is her emotional and ethical struggle that create the core action of the play. At times Evers is pulled into the world of testimony before scenes end or out of testimony after scenes begin resulting in a style and structure that are intentionally non-naturalistic. Evers should be kept in the eye of the audience whenever and as much as possible.

Note on scene transitions: The dialogue of MISS EVERS' BOYS is constructed to be played with minimal or no pause between scenes. This type of playing will add momentum to Evers' journey particularly in Act Two. Place indications are included in dialogue when needed (e.g., "Never thought I'd be standing in your office, Dr. Brodus."). Scene changes should be as seamless, brief and simple as possible.

Note on pronunciation: The "g" in "gillee" is soft and is sounded like the "j's" in "Jack and Jill." In terms of emphasis, "gillee" rhymes with "Billy."

Note on characters: It is important that Dr. Douglas and Dr. Brodus be represented as sympathetically as possible. If these characters are portrayed as easy villains the primary argument of the play (wrongdoing progressing in small and frequently unnoticed steps) falters and the relevance of the play to contemporary "right-seeming" research is lost.

ACT ONE

1932 — Contagion

Prologue: The Possom Hollow Schoolhouse, 1972.

1. The Possom Hollow Schoolhouse, 1932.
2. The Possom Hollow Schoolhouse, two months later.
3. The Possom Hollow Schoolhouse, one week later.
4. The Possom Hollow Schoolhouse, six months later.
5. The Office of Dr. Brodus, two weeks later.
6. The Possom Hollow Schoolhouse, two weeks later.
7. The Office of Dr. Brodus, three days later.
8. The Possom Hollow Schoolhouse, one week later.

ACT TWO

1946. 1972 — Progression and Endpoint

1. The Gillee and the Office of Dr. Brodus, 1946.
2. A Birmingham Rapid Treatment Center, one month later.
3. The Office of Dr. Brodus, the following week.
4. The Possom Hollow Schoolhouse, two weeks later.
5. The Possom Hollow Schoolhouse, three months later.
6. Memorial Hospital, four months later.
7. The Office of Dr. Brodus, two months later.
8. A field, two days later.

Epilogue: The Possom Hollow Schoolhouse, 1972.

MISS EVERS' BOYS

ACT ONE

Prologue

1972. Outside the Possom Hollow Schoolhouse. A crisp American flag and a printed sign are in evidence. The sign reads: "United States Senate Testimony Site; Location: (written in by hand) Possom Hollow School; Date: (written in by hand) April 24, 1972. During the following testimony we see Hodman, Ben, Caleb and Willie cautiously entering the shadows of the darkened schoolhouse not knowing what to expect. All except Ben have attended this school for various periods of time. They feel and look incongruous in the miniature schoolhouse setting. Hodman carries an empty metal oil drum supported by a sling over his shoulder. Ben carries a washboard with a kazoo and assorted bells fixed to the top (or a homemade washtub bass instrument). Caleb carries a harmonica embedded in a homemade, tin-can megaphone (or a metal string banjo). As the men enter they create long shadows in the schoolhouse. We hear gillee music increasing in volume as Evers speaks her testimony.

EVERS.   *(As testimony, fervently, each resolution more important than the previous one.)*
I solemnly pledge myself before God and in the presence
    of this assembly;
To pass my life in purity and to practice my profession
    faithfully;
To hold in confidence all matters revealed to me in the

practice of my calling;
To abstain from knowingly administering any harmful
medicine;
To do all in my power to maintain the standard of the
nursing profession;
To endeavor with loyalty to aid the physician in his work;
To devote myself to the welfare of those patients committed
to my care.

I've recited that pledge a thousand times, Senator. I know it by heart. *(Blackout on Evers. Music out. Flag and sign disappear. Lights up sharply on the men.)*

Scene 1

1932. Inside the Possom Hollow Schoolhouse. Early evening.

HODMAN. *(Troubled.)* Parakeet.

WILLIE. What?

HODMAN. Parakeet. He say I got bit by a parakeet.

CALEB. Who did?

HODMAN. Kirk up at the main house.

BEN. So what.

CALEB. What that white trash know.

HODMAN. He know enough to own your land and mine. Kirk say something, you do it.

CALEB. Do what?

HODMAN. Stay put. That's what. Stay put in this stinky schoolhouse 'til the government bad blood doctors come. That's what Kirk say.

BEN. *(Anxious.)* Doctor going to be here?

CALEB. How that doctor gonna know if you got bit by a parakeet?

HODMAN. Kirk say we gotta give our blood.

CALEB. Give blood?

HODMAN. That's how they know.

WILLIE. Not me. They ain't stickin' me.

CALEB. I ain't givin' up my blood, I'll tell you that.

HODMAN. Kirk says you have to.

CALEB. I hate that bastard.

BEN. Be quiet, Caleb.

CALEB. Why? No one around?

BEN. Feels to me like there is.

CALEB. Well, there ain't.

BEN. My neck is itching.

CALEB. Stop that talk.

BEN. Artone Green got swung up not two miles from here.

WILLIE. Don't be talking about that, Ben.

BEN. Well, my neck is itching.

15

HODMAN.   Then scratch it and be quiet.

CALEB.   Come on, let's get out of here. We'll do the gillee practicing over to my place.

HODMAN.   Kirk want us here.

CALEB.   *(Commanding.)* I say, "let's go." Now. *(Caleb begins moving toward the door.)*

HODMAN.   *(Stopping him, sharply.)* Kirk want us here. *(They stand, waiting.)*

WILLIE.   *(Concerned.)* Grandpa say they took his blood.... He was soft for a week.

HODMAN.   What you mean?

WILLIE.   He say that blood taking make it so he couldn't do nothing with no woman no how for no whole week.

BEN.   Not taking my blood then.

CALEB.   *(To Hodman.)* No one can make you give up your blood.

HODMAN.   Kirk can.

BEN.   If you want to keep farming.

CALEB.   Hell, I don't.

BEN.   What else you got? *(Caleb turns and starts to leave. Hodman sits.)*

HODMAN.   If you know what's good for you, you'll sit and wait and keep your mouth shut.

CALEB.   Not me. Come on, Ben, let's go to the Crimson.

BEN.   *(Sits.)* I'm too old to be fightin' that kind of fight, Caleb.

CALEB.   That man says jump, you jump.

BEN.   Might be nothin'. Might be over in an hour.

CALEB.   *(To Willie.)* What about you, Willie? *(Willie sits.)*

WILLIE.   I'm staying.

CALEB.   *(Caleb pounds long and angrily on the oil drum, yelling with unsuppressed rage.)* Jump, jump, jump, jump, jump, jump, juuuuump.

BEN.   Caleb, let's not be fighting a fight we ain't gonna be winning.

CALEB.   *(Disgusted.)* Man says jump, we all jump. *(He joins them. The four sit. And wait. Lights dim on men. Lights up on Evers.)*

EVERS.   *(As testimony.)* My father was a tall man. As a little girl, I would run Sunday mornings to watch him raise his arm high up over his head so that he could reach a tin can that he had hidden behind an oak crossbeam above the entranceway to our kitchen. "Money in the bank," he'd smile, rattling the tin can that held that week's addition to the household change. Then he'd lift me up in his arms so I could touch it too. On a Sunday morning the week of my fifth birthday, he held me up and as my hand touched the cool tin can I felt a tiny tremor in his arms. The next day, Monday, my father took to bed with a quiet cough. His temperature increased on Tuesday and Wednesday. Shaking and chills came Thursday. By Friday daybreak, my father, a man who could stand in his Sunday shoes and touch higher than the oak crossbeam at the entranceway to our kitchen, had passed on.... I remember crying when I was told that my father would not be playing with me again. That he was gone. Forever. "But what about after I wake up? After this night?" I didn't understand the word "forever." I just knew there was something keeping me from my father. Something I hated. "Pneumonia," they called it. I hated that "pneumonia" and I held that hate in the back of my mind waiting for the day when something would come along to destroy that "pneumonia" as easily as my father had swung me up in his arms the Sunday of my fifth birthday.... Twenty-three years later, in 1932, I was still waiting. *(Looking for something to do, Caleb pulls the rope going to the schoolbell; it sounds loudly.)*

HODMAN.   Quiet.

CALEB.   That's the same bell. *(He rings it again.)*

BEN.   Stop that.

CALEB.   *(As the sound dies.)* Same one.... I hated this place when I was seven. Don't look no better now. Where is everybody? How long we going to wait?

WILLIE.   *(At the blackboard.)* "Round b's, round p's, round o's." I remember this blackboard well enough.

BEN.   How much schooling you got?

WILLIE.   Two years.

CALEB.   *(Less cautious than the others; referring to a cracked and repaired section of a bench.)* Whooee. Look at it.

WILLIE.   What?

CALEB.   See how it's cracked and nailed down in two pieces?

HODMAN.   Yeah?

CALEB.   I did that.

BEN.   So what?

CALEB.   My head did that. In a fight with Stanley Dean. He grabbed me, swung me around, slammed my head and cracked this here board.

HODMAN.   What you do to him?

CALEB.   Look at here. See this bench? It used to be one foot longer. Stanley's head was harder than mine. It broke this board right off.... That was my best doing in this stinky schoolhouse. *(He sniffs.)* It smells. It smells the same. That's how I can remember so well. *(They all sniff.)*

WILLIE.   Yeah. yeah, it do. "Like green cabbage."

HODMAN.   *(Joins in, remembering how he used to describe it.)* "Like a dust sandwich."

CALEB.   *(Remembering how he used to describe it.)* "Like manure gravy."

BEN.   *(He doesn't understand.)* You boys is crazy.

WILLIE.   Miss Jane Teeters make you close your eyes, take a deep breath and write a "line of poetry?"

CALEB.   Yes, ma'am.

HODMAN.   She sure did.

WILLIE.   *(Sniffs once.)* "Like green cabbage." That was my line of poetry.

BEN.   *(Interrupting, angry.)* Schooling be good for kids nowadays. I never set foot in a school when I was young. And look what I've got. If I had children, I'd work 'til my overalls was quilted trying to save up the money to get them to college.

HODMAN.   What good it do? No jobs anyhow.

BEN.   You want them to sweat a farm out of hard-scrabble land for five cents cotton? Start with nothing. End with nothing.

WILLIE.   *(Sharp, determined.)* We're ending with something, Ben.

BEN. *(Challenging.)* What?

WILLIE. What you mean, what?

BEN. What?

WILLIE. You wait until Saturday, I'll show you what. *(Moving quickly to the blackboard he finds chalk and starts to write "Aspiration" on the blackboard.)* Caleb, Miss Teeters make you write this on the board until your hand ached? Ben, this means that you want to go somewhere and you're going to go there and there's nothing that's going to stop you. See, I got an "Aspiration" to go North. To win that gillee competition on Saturday and strut my way North into a club or something. I ain't ending up with nothing.

CALEB. That's good, Willie.

WILLIE. *(He starts dancing.)* From now until Saturday I don't sit down unless I have to or I'm too tired not to. *(Hodman and Caleb play a ragged supporting rhythm to Willie's dancing.)*

BEN. *(Increasingly afraid.)* Don't let them catch you dancing in here.

CALEB. We not children no more, Ben.

WILLIE. Come on, play a little for me, Ben.

BEN. Can't think straight. Feel watched.

WILLIE. Well, that Victrola we're gonna win, it ain't got to think straight. It do whatever we want.

BEN. *(Strongly, stopping them.)* Well, we ain't won it yet. *(Pause; they can't help but wonder if they are being watched.)*

WILLIE. *(Looking around.)* Gets spooky here at night.

HODMAN. The other day something come to me and said, just like somebody talking, "Corn bread is killing you." *(Referring to a necklace.)* That's why I started wearing this here mole's foot.

BEN. *(To Hodman.)* Can you write? Hodman?

HODMAN. What?

BEN. Can you write?

HODMAN. Sure.

BEN. Caleb?

CALEB. *(Going to the blackboard and finding chalk.)* Some. I was good with numbers. *(He writes "2 x 2" and then stops, challenging Hodman to answer.)* Two times two ...

HODMAN.   You didn't finish.

CALEB.   I'm waiting for you to tell me what to put down next.

HODMAN.   You started it. You finish it.

CALEB.   *(Holding up the chalk.)* Here. I bet you can't even write your own name.

HODMAN.   You'd lose.

CALEB.   Go on. Write it.

WILLIE.   I thought you said you could?

BEN.   You did say that.

HODMAN.   What about you, Ben. What about you?

BEN.   Me? *(He goes to the blackboard and writes a large "X".)* That's how I spell "Ben." And I ain't never had no need to spell it different.

HODMAN.   If I wrote it, you all wouldn't know how to read it.

WILLIE.   *(Who has written his first name on the blackboard.)* Here's mine.

CALEB.   *(Writes his first name.)* And mine.

HODMAN.   I can write. It's just going to take a little longer.

CALEB.   Why's that?

HODMAN.   Because I have a longer name.

CALEB.   Go on and write your name, Hodman. Write it.

HODMAN.   *(He goes to the blackboard and begins, then stops.)* This here chalk's no good.

WILLIE.   Here. *(He hands him another piece of chalk. Hodman begins struggling to write his first name. They all watch him.)*

CALEB.   *(Laughing at him.)* You don't have to invent the letter, Hodman, just write it. *(Hodman suddenly turns away from the blackboard.)*

HODMAN.   What's that?

CALEB.   What's what?

HODMAN.   I'm not joking. Somebody's coming.

BEN.   *(At window.)* A car. *(They are on guard expecting the worst; increasingly anxious. The following lines leading to Evers' entrance come out in a rush.)*

CALEB.   Must be Kirk.

WILLIE.   *(He stops dancing.)* Must be. *(They are uncertain what to do. Headlights momentarily shine through the window; the men involuntarily duck out of its path, frightened, hiding in the shadows of the schoolhouse.)*

BEN.   *(Suddenly to Hodman; pointing to the blackboard.)* Take that off there. *(Willie looks down the road. Hodman starts erasing the blackboard.)*

CALEB.   They ain't taking my blood.

HODMAN.   I wouldn't be here except Kirk want us to.

BEN.   *(Frightened.)* Who is it? Who's coming? *(Pointing to his "X".)* What you doing? Take that off of there.

WILLIE.   *(Searching.)* Look like a Chevy. With a rumble seat.

BEN.   You think it's a set up, Caleb?

CALEB.   *(Strong.)* Set up for what? We ain't important enough to be set up for nothing.

BEN.   I don't like dealing with white folks. Means nothing but trouble.

HODMAN.   You know what's good for you, you sit and keep your mouth shut.

WILLIE.   *(Still at the window.)* Somebody coming.

BEN.   You should have cleaned that board off better.

CALEB.   Sit down. *(They move quickly to sit down.)*

BEN.   *(Desperate; to Caleb who is nearest the blackboard.)* Take my mark off of there.

CALEB.   How's anyone going to know it's you, Ben?

BEN.   *(Ben rushes up to the board and using his hand as an eraser smudges his "X.")* I don't want to rile nobody.

CALEB.   Don't show them you afraid, Ben. Willie. You hear me, Hodman?

HODMAN.   Yes, I hear you. Now shut your mouth. *(Pause; they sit, waiting. Evers enters. The men involuntarily react to her entrance and stand. Rigid. Evers, not expecting anyone to be in the schoolhouse yet, is startled.)*

EVERS.   Oh. Oh. Lord, oh me. *(Getting her breath.)* Oh. Oh, Lord. Hmm ... I must remind you of Miss Jane Teeters. You're all standing there all straight and fine. *(Recovering, amused.)* Lord, oh me. Oh.

CALEB.   *(Cutting her off.)* Mr. Kirk with you?

EVERS.   Who?

CALEB.   Mr. Kirk. White boss man.

EVERS.   No. Just me. No white man.

CALEB.   Glad to hear that.

BEN.   Me too.

HODMAN.   You sure?

EVERS.   Yes, sir.

HODMAN.   *(The men begin to relax.)* How you know about Miss Teeters?

EVERS.   She came down to Tuskegee twice for help with her boys. She's pretty old now.

HODMAN.   She pretty old then.

BEN.   Hush up. Don't sass the lady.

EVERS.   Oh, no offense taken. But thank you, Mr...?

BEN.   Ben. Ben Washington.

EVERS.   Well, thank you, Mr. Washington.

HODMAN.   I know you. You Nurse Evers?

EVERS.   Yes, I am.

HODMAN.   Son of a gun. You delivered up my nephew by Possom Glade. The Parker place.

EVERS.   Yes, I recall. The same night the wind blew the water tower over in Dean.

HODMAN.   That's it. That was one ugly baby but I don't blame you.

EVERS.   I'm glad to hear it.

WILLIE.   You been nursin' up by Chattam and all round Macon?

EVERS.   Off and on for eight years now.

WILLIE.   I've heard of you. My friend, Jody, she mentioned you to me. She said you got this green Chevrolet and the people all line up for their doctorin' soon as they see the dust you done kicked up two miles away. Is that the car?

EVERS.   Same one.

BEN.   *(Remembering.)* You the hat nurse?

EVERS.   They call me that?

BEN.   Yes, ma'am.

EVERS.   I figure you change your hat, you change the top of your world.

BEN.   *(Enjoying her.)* Yes, ma'am.

WILLIE.   Nice to meet you. I'm Willie Johnson, with an "h."
And this here is Hodman Bryan. *(Hodman nods "hello".)*
CALEB.   I'm Caleb Humphries. *(Evers takes out paper and sup-
plies to write down the patients' names.)* Nurse Evers ...
EVERS.   Yes, Mr. Humphries.
CALEB.   Kirk send you here to take blood?
EVERS.   No, Mr. Humphries, Kirk didn't send me. Ain't no
white man sent me. A colored man, a fine and important
man, Dr. Eugene Brodus, up at Tuskegee, he sent me. And
he told me to wear my Goodnews Hat. And to offer you all
free doctorin'. *(The men are suspicious.)*
BEN.   Free?
CALEB.   You say, "free."
EVERS.   Yes, I did. The doctorin's free and just as fine as
any you can get with any kind of money.
HODMAN.   I don't want my blood took. I got ... obliga-
tions. I don't care about "free." And I didn't get bit by no
parakeet. None of us did.
EVERS.   Parakeet?
HODMAN.   Kirk up at the main house said you'd see if we
got bit by the parakeet that causes bad blood.
EVERS.   Oh. That man was wrong.
HODMAN.   I knew it. I knew it.
EVERS.   He meant "spirochete." That's the germ that causes
bad blood.
HODMAN.   I didn't get bit by nothing.
EVERS.   Well now, that's hard to tell. Sometimes you don't
know —
HODMAN.   We know — *(The men agree.)*
EVERS.   *(Cutting them off.)* Until it's too late. *(Selling the idea.)*
But the government, the United States government I'm talk-
ing about now, in Washington, is sending us the best medi-
cine to treat anyone in this county that needs it. Even if
you're poor, if you got bad blood, you're going to get the
chance to be treated. Now that's something. And that's what
I drove all this way to tell you.
BEN.   We never got free doctorin' before.
CALEB.   How come they never interested before?

EVERS.   Well, they're interested now. And we're not going to get nothing unless we grab onto what's being offered and what's being offered is better than anything we ever got.

CALEB.   Why us?

EVERS.   *(Laughing, amused.)* You are a suspicious man, aren't you?

CALEB.   *(Enjoying her enjoyment.)* Just like to know where in the row the rocks are hiding. So I don't break the plow.

EVERS.   You're a careful farmer?

CALEB.   When I have to be.

EVERS.   But you still run over some rocks, don't you?

CALEB.   Not often.

EVERS.   But sometimes?

CALEB.   Sometimes. Sure.

EVERS.   *(Lightly, she's trapped him.)* See. Sometimes you got to take a chance or else you get nothing.

HODMAN.   *(Enjoying the dueling.)* Oooo, you tell him, Nurse Evers.

EVERS.   Now, you all hear me good now: we got a chance to get people well on a bushel basketful of government money. That's a chance we got to take. *(Silence.)*

BEN.   I don't got bad blood. But I got bad rheumatism.

HODMAN.   Just put a knife under your pillow every night like I told you. That'll cut the pain.

BEN.   I have been.

HODMAN.   Like I told you? With the blade toward your feet.

BEN.   Yes, that's what I been doing.

HODMAN.   Well, you keep doing it then. That'll work.

EVERS.   You into cures, Mr. Bryan?

HODMAN.   Yes, ma'am. Come from a family of healers. What you think of that knife cure? Worked fine for my wife.

EVERS.   Well, I never used it myself. But I think if you know something that helps you, you know a good thing.

HODMAN.   Hear what she say, Ben?

BEN.   Stop strutting, Hodman. I hear her.

WILLIE.   Nurse Evers?

EVERS.   Yes?

WILLIE.   What you mean "until it's too late?" You said we

might not know "until it's too late".

EVERS. That spirochete germ can make trouble with your heart. And with your head. And with your muscles and movement. It can make it so you don't know where your feet are going. You can hardly walk. You shuffle.

WILLIE. That's bad.

EVERS. It can kill you.

WILLIE. *(Quietly, to Caleb.)* I told you we ought to get us some life insurance.

CALEB. You ain't sick. Not the way you dance. *(A momentary dance suddenly erupts between the two men.)*

EVERS. *(Cutting them off.)* But the sneaky thing about bad blood is that you all might have it right now and don't even know it.

HODMAN. I don't want my blood took. I'm still young. I got a wife. I've got obligations. We all do. Even Ben.

BEN. What you mean "even Ben", Hodman?

EVERS. Obligations?

HODMAN. To my wife, I mean. You know.... Family obligations. So I just can't have my blood took.

EVERS. Oh. Well, I think I understand your concern, Mr. Bryan. But I can assure you that taking your blood won't interfere with your obligations.

CALEB. That ain't what Willie's grandpa said. He said it interfered with his obligations for a week.

EVERS. You know Fred Milsen down by Alma?

CALEB. The sawmill foreman?

EVERS. Same one. Now he got seven children going on eight and he's been giving his blood for 6 years. His obligations been going fine. Both in the short run and the long run.

HODMAN. I hope you right.

EVERS. I am and I wouldn't say it if it wasn't so. *(Ready to put down his name.)* Mr. Washington?

CALEB. *(Interrupting.)* Why the government helping us all of a sudden? They got a war coming on or something?

EVERS. No such thing. The government got a new point of view on things.

CALEB.   What's that?

EVERS.   A people point of view. They want to get rid of all the sickness around here. They interested.

CALEB.   The government interested in us?

EVERS.   *(Matching him.)* The Public Health Service is interested and they are part of the government. *(Ready to write down his name.)* Mr. Washington?

BEN.   You be our nurse?

EVERS.   Yes, sir.

CALEB.   *(Sharply.)* Ben.

BEN.   What?

CALEB.   Don't sign nothing until you know what you're signing.

BEN.   I know.

CALEB.   *(Interrupting before Ben can say anything else.)* I don't remember getting nothing free before. And we all healthy, Nurse Evers.

EVERS.   Well, you still going to get free doctorin', Mr. Humphries. Even if you're healthy.

HODMAN.   *(Positive.)* That sounds nice, Caleb.

EVERS.   Well, how about you, Mr. Bryan?

CALEB.   Hold on, Hodman.

EVERS.   *(Direct, serious, strong.)* This is a good thing. We don't get a lot of chances around here to say, "no", to a good thing. *(Pause. Silence.)*

BEN.   *(Breaking the silence.)* Where you from, Miss Evers?

EVERS.   Originally from Rynert, Mr. Washington.

BEN.   You gotta call me "Ben" or I won't know who you're talking to.

WILLIE.   Me neither.

HODMAN.   Same for me.

BEN.   We all can't be "Ben."

EVERS.   *(Laughing.)* All right. That will be fine. Ben.

WILLIE.   You got kin folks up there?

EVERS.   All over Macon and in Tuscaloosa. But no direct kin.

HODMAN.   You ain't married?

EVERS.   No. Been too busy.

CALEB.   Doing what?

EVERS.   Supporting myself, Mr. Humphries. Tuskegee nursing school. Worked nursing for the county until the really bad times hit in '30.

BEN.   What you been doing since then?

EVERS.   Domestic work when I could get it.

BEN.   Domestic work?... You a nurse.

EVERS.   That's what Dr. Eugene Brodus up at Tuskegee thought too. So when the government started this program, he called me and now I'm back to nursing.

BEN.   That's only right.

WILLIE.   *(An important connection.)* Well. *(Addressing everyone in the room.)* Looks like we all got something in common.

EVERS.   What's that?

WILLIE.   Well, we a group. The four of us.

EVERS.   What do you mean?

WILLIE.   *(Doing a few quick steps which the others support.)* You looking at the next winners of the Macon County Victrola Gillee Competition come this Saturday.

EVERS.   Saturday?

WILLIE.   Yes, ma'am. And you know why we're going to win?

EVERS.   Because you all the best. I can tell that by looking at you.

WILLIE.   I am and we are. That's true too. But see this here's why. *(Goes to the blackboard.)* Can you make this out?

EVERS.   No I can't.

WILLIE.   I put this here. It say, "Aspiration". Like when you was doing that domestic cleaning 'cause you wanted to get back to your nursing. You had to work, right?

EVERS.   Right.

WILLIE.   Work hard. Real hard. That's "Aspiration". You got it. And we got it too. That's what we all got in common. *(The other men agree.)*

EVERS.   *(Sincerely complimented.)* Why, thank you. That's a fine word.

CALEB.   Willie here's the best double fly stepper around. *(Willie does the step.)*

WILLIE.   *(Demonstrating.)* See that. *(With delight.)* Damn.... Sorry, Nurse Evers. I say "damn" 'cause I work with horses.

EVERS.   That's all right. A once in a while "damn" is all right with me.

WILLIE.   Now here's a lady who understands gilleein'.

EVERS.   And horses.

WILLIE.   (Laughing.) And horses, yes ma'am.

BEN.   I play a mean washboard, Nurse Evers.

HODMAN.   I slaps a beat.

EVERS.   (To Caleb.) You?

CALEB.   I bend the notes.

EVERS.   Well, you all are something I'll have to see.

BEN.   I'd like that.

WILLIE.   You're invited. Anytime.

HODMAN.   You watch that gillee, just as soon as they turn those headlights from the cars on us, you got to jump up and screech and scream so we win. (The men laugh enjoying the thought.)

EVERS.   (Laughing.) Lord, oh lord. How you getting there Saturday?

HODMAN.   Two feet. One racing the other.

EVERS.   I could get the government to pay for your transportation to that competition.

WILLIE.   How's that?

EVERS.   I could drive you there. First, I take you over to the hospital. Get your free tests and your free hot lunch.

HODMAN.   Free lunch?

EVERS.   That's right.

HODMAN.   This sound better and better.

EVERS.   Then I'll drive you back, after the competition.

WILLIE.   We get picked up just like we had our own chauffeur or something.

HODMAN.   We a regular lodge with our own limousine.

EVERS.   That's it. What you all call yourselves?

WILLIE.   We hadn't thought of that?

HODMAN.   Fellas from Birmingham are called The Juicer Boys. (Ben whispers to Evers.)

CALEB.   And those from Catchim, call themselves the Wagonsfull.

EVERS.   (Laughing, to Ben.) My Lord, you crazy. But I'd be

proud and I'd be shouting you on.

CALEB. What you got, Ben?

BEN. Straight from Possom Hollow: "Miss Evers' Boys." *(The men relish Evers' appreciation and their newfound status.)*

WILLIE. *(Using a bench and desk he gets ready to gillee.)* Jackspring. And play it hot. *(He starts a rhythm.)* How you like this sound?

EVERS. Sounds like a skip time to me.

WILLIE. Whooeee. Listen to her. *(Clapping her hands Evers changes the rhythm, challenging Willie to keep up with her now dancing feet. He does so with the enjoyment of a man who knows he has a gift. Evers' enthusiasm is apparent. The men take out their instruments and begin to rev up. They heartily enjoy Evers.)*

EVERS. *(Impressed.)* Look at you.

WILLIE. Look at you. *(The men laugh.)*

EVERS. Dance 'em down, Willie Johnson.

WILLIE. I can't hear you, Nurse Evers.

EVERS. *(Loud.)* Dance 'em all the way down, Willie Johnson.

BEN. We're gonna do you proud, Nurse Evers.

EVERS. You're going to do me in, Ben.

WILLIE. Let's do the "All Go." ... One, two, three, four — *(They start to play together. We hear the following lines over the music and dance. Willie encourages Evers to join in the celebration. To the men, a rhythmic chant.)* All, go.

OTHER MEN. *(The men answer.)* Jump, jump.

WILLIE. You all, go.

OTHER MEN. Jump, jump.

WILLIE. You all, GO.

ALL FOUR MEN. Jump, jump. OHHHHH. *(The dance begins.)*

WILLIE. *(After a few steps, suddenly, stopping.)* Hold it. Hold it now. You all gonna have to play faster. See, I'm just doing it "turtle style," Nurse Evers.

EVERS. *(Silence. Evers looks at the men.)* You men are winners. That's easy to see. But you got to stay healthy to win. You got to stay healthy. If you're going to win. *(She takes out the sign-up paper. Pause.)*

BEN. Nurse Evers —

EVERS.   Yes, Ben?

BEN.   *(Proud.)* Put me down.

WILLIE.   *(After a moment.)* There's an "h" in my name.

HODMAN.   I'll go along with the others. *(Pause.)*

BEN.   Come on, Caleb. Don't keep the lady waiting.

CALEB.   All right. You can put my name down.

EVERS.   *(Simply.)* Fine ... *(Brighter, a challenge.)* Come on now, burst this old schoolhouse with all your gilleein'.

WILLIE.   You wait 'til Saturday. We're gonna explode. One, two, three, four — *(They play fast and furious. The brief dance and music quickly build to a climax. Suddenly the men freeze in a tableau before the dance is finished. Evers turns toward the audience.)*

EVERS.   Those men won that Victrola. Hands down. *(Sound of train whistle as Dr. Douglas enters. He is wearing a fine suit and carrying a new doctor's bag.)* Two months later, the doctors arrived. *(Another train whistle. Set and light change. The men move into the new scene.)*

Scene 2

1932. Outside the Possom Hollow Schoolhouse. Two months later. Ben, Caleb, and Willie wait in line as Douglas, who is taking notes on a clipboard, is confronted by Hodman. It should be clear that the argument between the two has been continuing for some time. The other men and Evers watch.

HODMAN.   *(Stepping forward toward Douglas, challenging, as the other men and Evers watch.)* What you mean, "anemia"? No one ever ask me that before.

DOUGLAS.   It means your hemoglobin is low.

HODMAN.   What you mean "hemoglobin"? *(Insulted.)* And what you mean "low"?

EVERS.   Doctor?

DOUGLAS.   Yes?

EVERS.   *(Quietly, prompting Douglas.)* "Low blood." That's the Miss Evers' Version.

DOUGLAS. *(To Hodman.)* Do you have "low blood"?
HODMAN. Well, why didn't you say so, Doc. Say it like it
is. "Low blood." Say it straight ... *(Answering the question.)* No.
(Hodman moves back in line as Ben comes forward.)
DOUGLAS. Mr. Washington? *(To Ben.)* Are you potent?
BEN. *(Not knowing the word.)* Potent?
DOUGLAS. Are you sexually active?... Do you have carnal
relations?... Can you ... *(To Evers, quietly.)* The Miss Evers'
Version?
EVERS. Hot blood, doctor.
DOUGLAS. I'll bet you have hot blood, don't you?
HODMAN. *(As the others react.)* You'd lose.
WILLIE. Yes, you would.
BEN. He'd win. I got "good blood."
WILLIE. Then I got "extra good." *(He does a quick step.)*
BEN. This man's all right. He knows "hot blood" when he
sees it. *(The men enjoy this interchange.)*
DOUGLAS. *(Direct, caring.)* Gentlemen, please.... There's a
germ, the spirochete, that infects the genitals resulting in a
painless, unnoticed, temporary but highly contagious penile
ulceration that disappears as the disease becomes non-contagious or latent, a latency of up to thirty years until, finally,
infested with the treponema microbe, the cardiovascular and
nervous systems disintegrate and collapse. *(Pause; no reaction
from the men.)*
EVERS. *(Coming to Douglas' rescue.)* By too much frolickin'
you can get a dangerous sore down below on your private
parts and through that sore a bug can crawl inside you and
you won't even know it. And then that bug goes to sleep for
twenty or thirty years so it's not hurting anybody but you.
Because when it wakes up, you can't walk, you can't breathe,
you can't think. That's bad blood. That's what you got. *(The
men are impressed. To Douglas.)* Now they understand, doctor.
Now they'll show up for treatment. Use that chapter and
verse and you'll do fine.
DOUGLAS. Nurse Evers?
EVERS. Yes, sir.
DOUGLAS. Don't go away. *(Set and lights change to indicate*

*passage of time. The men exit singing "Children, Don't Be Afraid."** *Willie remains behind. He begins practicing a gillee step.)*

EVERS. *(As testimony.)* 626 were positive for syphilis. Including Miss Evers' Boys. Yes, there were other places, colored and white, with just as much syphilis. But the government, Senator, chose Macon County. And when the government made that choice, well, I just figured our turn for good times had finally come…. The following week we tested blood and we began treatment for those men: a two-year course of mercury salve body rubs and injections of arsenic. That was the best treatment available at that time. Fifty-five per cent effective. It could cure you. If it didn't kill you first. *(Light change. Evers crosses to prepare instruments for blood drawing as Douglas enters. Willie continues practicing.)*

Scene 3

1932. Outside the Possom Hollow Schoolhouse. One week later. Willie is practicing knee drops. He is separate from Evers who is preparing instruments for blood drawing. Douglas approaches Willie with a tourniquet and needle.

DOUGLAS. *(Approaching with the tourniquet, confident.)* If you'll just roll up your sleeve, Mr. Johnson, I'll draw that blood. Quick and easy.
WILLIE. *(Willie does some knee drops. He knows Douglas is there and is intentionally ignoring him. There is anger in his dance.)* One, two, drop, drop. One, drop.
DOUGLAS. I was just asking a question. A medical question, Mr. Johnson … I never said your grandfather had bad blood.
WILLIE. Grandpa couldn't see a cow in daylight, but he sure could listen. He'd listen real hard to the click clackin'

---

* See Special Note on Songs and Recordings on copyright page.

of my feet and he could tell what they was doing. Just like he could see them.

DOUGLAS. *(After a moment.)* It's possible that your grandfather did not have bad blood.

WILLIE. I don't think he did.

DOUGLAS. I was just asking a standard question, Mr. Johnson. I ask everyone the same question.

WILLIE. *(With determination and some anger, moving away from and deliberately ignoring Douglas.)* One, two, drop, drop. One drop, two. *(Douglas moves to Evers for assistance.)*

EVERS. Some people grate on each other, Dr. Douglas.

DOUGLAS. I didn't say his grandfather had bad blood.

EVERS. Well, that's how he took it.

DOUGLAS. Willie inherited the disease. From his grandfather to his mother to him. It's fact.

EVERS. Dr. Douglas, these men may not be interested in the facts ... as you see them.

DOUGLAS. *(After a moment.)* I've always been a good medicine doctor. I've never been a great patient doctor.

EVERS. I believe you're a kind of person who gets something done, if he really wants to do it.

DOUGLAS. I want to do it.

EVERS. Then talk to him. About more than just business. Show him you're interested.

DOUGLAS. I am interested.

EVERS. I know you are. But he doesn't.... Talk personal talk. Respectful. Man to man. And let the "facts" go on vacation for a while.

DOUGLAS. *(Agreeable.)* All right.... All right, I'll do just that. *(He looks at Willie but does not move.)*

EVERS. *(After a moment.)* Go on.

DOUGLAS. *(Like jumping into cold water.)* All right. Here I go. *(He doesn't move.)*

EVERS. Go. *(Evers returns to her work. She remains onstage but at a distance.)*

DOUGLAS. *(Douglas moves toward Willie who continues to ignore him. Evers watches from a distance. Finally, Douglas finds something to say.)* Mr. Johnson, you're going to crack your cartilage.

WILLIE.   My what?

DOUGLAS.   You're going to ruin your knees.

WILLIE.   I got no choice. The Wagonsfull got Sam Heart dancing. He does knee drops from two feet. I gotta do them from four feet to win. And I got to do them now. *(Douglas watches.)* Bet you you never seen no step like that before, have you?

DOUGLAS.   Actually I have seen something similar to that.

WILLIE.   *(Skeptical.)* Oh, you have?

DOUGLAS.   Something like it.

WILLIE.   Done as fine as that.

DOUGLAS.   Probably not.

WILLIE.   Where?

DOUGLAS.   Harlem. The Cotton Club.

WILLIE.   *(Disbelieving.)* You're lying.

DOUGLAS.   No. No, I'm not.

WILLIE.   Why would you go there?

DOUGLAS.   Why not?

WILLIE.   Because you a ... it's not your kind of music that's why not.

DOUGLAS.   I like the sound of it.

WILLIE.   Oh, you do? *(Skeptical, testing.)* Who's your favorite?

DOUGLAS.   Jelly Roll Morton's —

WILLIE.   *(Finishing for him, skeptical.)* Red Hot Peppers. Who else?

DOUGLAS.   Fletcher Henderson. Duke Ellington. King Oliver's Creole Jazz Band.

WILLIE.   Red Onion Jazz Babies?

DOUGLAS.   Yes, I like them. Very much.

WILLIE.   *(Amazed.)* You had your feet in the Cotton Club.

DOUGLAS.   Yes.

WILLIE.   Who you seen dance there?

DOUGLAS.   Ruby Blue.

WILLIE.   *(With growing excitement.)* You seen Ruby Blue?

DOUGLAS.   Yes.

WILLIE.   Did he scatter and then leap-turn right? Tell me the most exciting thing he did.

DOUGLAS.   I can't remember.

WILLIE. You're not trying.

DOUGLAS. It was years ago.

WILLIE. You see my knees. You want me to bust up my "cartriges" or what?

DOUGLAS. I don't remember him, Mr. Johnson.

WILLIE. You're not trying. Now try. *(He starts knee dropping.)*

DOUGLAS. All right. *(Willie stops.)* He had a smooth sort of spin. *(Willie does it automatically.)*

WILLIE. No. *(Disappointed.)* I got that already. *(Demonstrates.)* Something else.

DOUGLAS. He had some stairs.

WILLIE. I got stairs already. *(Willie demonstrates.)* What he do with his stairs? That's what I gotta know.

DOUGLAS. When he'd dance one foot would be doing one thing on one step and another would be doing something else on another step lower down.

WILLIE. Doing what?

DOUGLAS. The front foot was doing a high step ...

WILLIE. Kinda ... *(Working it out.)* like this?

DOUGLAS. Yes.

WILLIE. What about the back foot?

DOUGLAS. The back foot was traveling along very smoothly.

WILLIE. *(Showing.)* How's this?

DOUGLAS. Yes. That would be an approximation.

WILLIE. *(Demanding more.)* That's not special enough.

DOUGLAS. But both feet were working the different rhythms at the same time. And he'd use the stairs.

WILLIE. Like a different person dancing on each leg?

DOUGLAS. Yes.

WILLIE. Now, that's nice. That's new. *(He finds a place with different levels.)* Kind of like this. *(Getting excited, he experiments with the step.)* What about the arms?

DOUGLAS. The arms were moving back and forth.

WILLIE. How?

DOUGLAS. Well. Sort of ... *(He tries to demonstrate the movement. He can move well but feels uncomfortable doing it.)*

WILLIE. Pumping. That's pumping. What rhythm? What was that rhythm?

DOUGLAS. *(Douglas, uncomfortable, tries to remember the rhythm and starts to repeat it.)* Da, da, da-da-da ... I can't remember.
WILLIE. *(Still experimenting.)* Like "da, da, da, da."
DOUGLAS. Yes, da, da, da.
WILLIE. What was he doing with his head?
DOUGLAS. Moving it. Back and forth.
WILLIE. How?
DOUGLAS. *(Having gone this far he knows he has to finish; Douglas demonstrates bobbing his head sharply to the music.)* Da, da, da, da. *(He repeats the rhythm. As they dance together, Douglas relaxes more and almost begins to enjoy himself. He dances gracefully, in his own style.)* Da, da, da ...
WILLIE. You're good, Dr. Douglas. You do some more of that, Dr. Douglas, we'll get you in. *(Building; determined.)* Now: Da, da, da, da. *(Willie puts it all together.)* "One, two, three ... da, da, da, da. *(He turns, skips and starts again using the levels.)* "One, two, three, da, da, da, da." *(He looks at Douglas and starts using his head and smiling, exuberant.)* Da, DA. My legs are feeling good. *(Evers is watching from the instrument table. Willie builds the rhythm to completion, finishes the dance with a flourish and sits, triumphant. He has learned what he set out to learn.)* Now, that's nice ... *(After a moment.)* I've never worked so close with a whi — *(He catches himself.)*
DOUGLAS. *(Helping Willie out of his embarrassment.)* A doctor, before?
WILLIE. Yes.
DOUGLAS. And I've never worked so close with a —
WILLIE. *(Teasing, enjoying their shared humor.)* A farmer?
DOUGLAS. Yes. A farmer. And where are the other "farmers"?
WILLIE. They're coming but they figure they don't got bad blood.
DOUGLAS. No?
WILLIE. They figure they don't got no blood with you all taking so much. *(In high spirits, calling to Evers.)* You know this man's been to the Cotton Club. You see him dance?
EVERS. I watched Dr. Douglas dance out of the corner of my disbelief. *(Laughing.)* Lord, oh me.

WILLIE. *(Joining her enjoyment.)* I didn't believe it myself....
Dr. Douglas.

EVERS. *(Impressed, to Douglas.)* Dr. Douglas .... *(Douglas appreciates the roundabout compliment; he goes to pick up the blood drawing equipment.)* You're feeling good, aren't you, Willie?

WILLIE. Like I got me a winning step for sure. That's a nice feeling. *(Douglas looks at Willie. Willie looks at Douglas and then crosses to him for the blood drawing. Evers moves in to help.)*

DOUGLAS. It will be quick and easy, Willie.

WILLIE. Can't be too quick and easy for me. *(Willie holds out his arm to Douglas. Douglas begins to draw Willie's blood.)* You got life insurance, Dr. Douglas?

DOUGLAS. What?

WILLIE. Life insurance.

DOUGLAS. No.

WILLIE. You don't? If you die, how you going to get buried? How could you pay for it?

DOUGLAS. It wouldn't cost that much.

WILLIE. My grandpa, he had insurance and he missed one payment and the Union Life took his insurance away and we couldn't even get him a decent coffin to be buried good in. We buried him in a feed sack. *(The blood drawing is finished.)*

DOUGLAS. There we are. Quick and easy.

WILLIE. I got to get me some life insurance, Dr. Douglas. Something I can depend on. To get buried good. *(Louder so Evers can hear; proud.)* This is some fine treatment you all giving us. Free of charge. *(Teasing.)* Now how about some life insurance courtesy of the United States government? Nothing to pay. Guaranteed. That be nice, wouldn't it, Nurse Evers?

EVERS. *(Playing along.)* What else you want, Willie?

WILLIE. Wouldn't mind if these gillee contests would offer up a fancy coffin as a prize. Then, of course, all four of us would have to die at once. *(Lights change to indicate the passage of time. The men enter singing "Travellin' Shoes"* accompanied by Victrola music. Hodman carries the prize Victrola over his head, high*

---

* See Special Note on Songs and Recordings on copyright page.

37

and proud. The men move into a line in front of the school and begin to massage each other's backs with mercury salve supplied by Evers from a large, white jar. She massages the last man in line. After the song ends, the men work to the music from the Victrola. Douglas watches.)

Scene 4

1932. Outside the Possom Hollow Schoolhouse. Six months later. Celebration. The men are massaging each other's backs with mercury. Evers guides them. The Victrola is playing. Douglas watches.

DOUGLAS.   What's going on?

EVERS.   Treatment. Mercury treatment. "Miss Evers' Style." *(To the men.)* Rub hard now. The Macon County Victrola Gillie Competition champions got to work. Squeeze that mercury into those muscles 'til they yell —

MEN.   *(All together, enjoying themselves, a shout.)* "Please!"

EVERS.   *(Miss Evers passes out more salve.)* Here you are now. Willie, go crank up that champion Victrola.

WILLIE.   Yes, ma'am. I just love the feeling of being able to hear music just by moving a needle. *(He turns the handle on the Victrola.)* And thanks for the new record, Dr. Douglas.

DOUGLAS.   How'd you break the Charleston Rag record?

WILLIE.   We didn't break it. *(Enjoying himself.)* We wore it out. *(Music starts; Willie looks at Douglas.)*

DOUGLAS.   *(Guessing, to Willie.)* The Red Onion Jazz Babies?

WILLIE.   Yes, sir. That's it. This man is right on the money.

HODMAN.   *(Interrupting, to Ben.)* Why do I always get stuck with you? I got obligations, you know. Rub harder. Ouch.

BEN.   That hard enough?

HODMAN.   Hey, don't shred me.

EVERS.   *(Enjoying herself.)* Lord, oh lord. You men are feeling frisky.

HODMAN.   Hot blood. *(The others agree.)*

BEN. *(Delighted.)* That's it.

EVERS. *(Enjoying herself; the men respond with ad libs to her observations.)* And you look good. Just like you should. Every one of you. You look healthy. *(Sharp silence and freeze. Tableau. Music out. Light up on Evers. Downlight on the men. Evers looks at them for a moment and then speaks to the audience, as testimony.)* Those first six months ... those men were winning every which way. Until the government pulled the string and the bottom fell out. *(Set change. The men exit. Dr. Brodus enters. Douglas crosses to Brodus' office as the set changes around him and the dialogue continues. Evers follows him.)*

Scene 5

1932. Memorial Hospital. The office of Dr. Eugene Brodus. Evers waits, listening. Two weeks later.

DOUGLAS. *(As if continuing an argument.)* There's no more money. It's as simple as that.

BRODUS. And if it were Manhattan and not Macon.

DOUGLAS. Dr. Brodus, I'm just telling you what I've been told to tell you. Washington tells me. I tell you. I'm as disappointed and frustrated as you are. I've given six months to this treatment program.

BRODUS. Yes, you have. *(Polite but cool.)* Thank you.

DOUGLAS. *(Stung.)* I'm just reminding you whose side I'm on.

BRODUS. *(Even more polite.)* Thank you, then. For reminding me.

DOUGLAS. Thousands of patients. Each patient requiring forty injections over two years.... *(Calming himself.)* Dr. Brodus, it's simply too much disease for the budget.

BRODUS. Those patients need that treatment.

DOUGLAS. Yes, sir, they do. Of course, they do.... And no one is going to get it for them, if we don't.

BRODUS.   We.

DOUGLAS.   Yes, sir. We. You and I and Nurse Evers and every person working on this project, and all those patients, all of us; we're all hanging onto Washington's attention by a single thread.

BRODUS.   And that thread is...?

DOUGLAS.   A suggestion. Just a suggestion. A temporary solution. A way to keep Washington's attention. A way to salvage this situation until Washington appropriates more funds.

BRODUS.   To continue treatment?

DOUGLAS.   Yes, sir. To continue treatment for those men. *(Sincere, dedicated.)* I believe that what we have here, in Macon County, is an extraordinary opportunity to catalogue the effects of untreated syphilis in the Negro.

BRODUS.   Untreated syphilis?

DOUGLAS.   We have a perfect laboratory here: a fixed population, virtually untreated disease. A study could be created and carried out with minimal expense. And it would be the most important study of its kind ever conducted. More important than the Oslo research because we'd be dealing with living patients not paper records.

EVERS.   Oslo?

DOUGLAS.   Nurse Evers, in Oslo, Norway, they studied the autopsy records of three hundred Caucasian patients who had died from untreated syphilis. To see what the disease had done to them. They studied the Caucasian. I believe the Negro should have a chance to be studied too.... That's my suggestion.

EVERS.   Those patients need medicine.

DOUGLAS.   And we are the only people who can get it for them. But we've got only one thing on our side, Nurse Evers: the disease itself. We follow these patients for six months. We catalogue what this disease untreated does to them. And then we let the facts speak for themselves. The Public Health Service could use those facts to educate, to motivate, to create new priorities. New money. For treatment. Not just for our patients but for every syphilitic in the country. A revolution in health care. *(Dedicated.)* And, Dr. Brodus, our research could prove conclusively if the disease differentiates along racial lines.

BRODUS.   What if it proves that Negro and Caucasian are equal? That the disease affects both races in exactly the same way? How would Washington feel about that suggestion?

DOUGLAS.   *(Matching him.)* Dr. Brodus, it doesn't matter how they'd feel, does it? If that data came from the best damned study ever done.

BRODUS.   *(Considering as he works on a tabulation.)* The high and mighty Dame Syphilis: the Italians called it the "French disease," the French called it the "Neopolitan disease," the Russians called it the "Polish disease." Do you know what they're all calling it now, up there in Washington?

DOUGLAS.   No, sir.

BRODUS.   Come now, Dr. Douglas, what are they all calling it now?

DOUGLAS.   *(Trapped.)* "The Negro disease."

BRODUS.   That's right. That's what they're calling it. But that's not what I call it. I call it, "God's disease." God has given it to man. To all men. Equal ...

DOUGLAS.   Yes, sir. I agree. Yes, sir. Yes. And we could prove that. Once and for all we could prove that what the disease does, it does to all of us, colored and white.

BRODUS.   You know what else they say up there, in Washington?

DOUGLAS.   No, sir.

BRODUS.   *(A hint and a challenge.)* "Money," Dr. Douglas, "money."

DOUGLAS.   *(Facing the challenge.)* "Don't throw white money —

BRODUS.   *(Finishing it for him.)* — after a colored man's disease."

DOUGLAS.   *(An admission and a challenge.)* That's right. That's what else they're saying.... Now are we going to let that kind of talk stand, Dr. Brodus, or are we going to fight it?

BRODUS.   *(After a moment.)* What would your role be, Dr. Douglas?

DOUGLAS.   I'd coordinate all the data and come down pe-

riodically for examinations. Liaison between Washington and
Macon.

BRODUS. Physician and scientist.

DOUGLAS. Yes.

BRODUS. That can be a uneasy combination.

DOUGLAS. Isn't that how you see yourself?

BRODUS. I'm a skeptic, Dr. Douglas. I'm the Voltaire of
pelvic literature.

DOUGLAS. You have some doubts?

BRODUS. Yes, I do. Always.... Would Washington match
Oslo?

DOUGLAS. I've already spoken with them.... Washington
needs your help, Dr. Brodus.

BRODUS. I see.... *(A change.)* The Negro must be studied
in exactly the same way they study the white. Periodic examinations —

DOUGLAS. Yes, sir.

BRODUS. X-rays?

DOUGLAS. Of course, yes. And blood work.

BRODUS. And spinal taps. Just like Oslo?

DOUGLAS. *(Dealing.)* Just like Oslo. Dr. Brodus, every patient in our study would have a spinal tap to test for neuro-
logic syphilis. Equal.

BRODUS. *(Considering.)* Six months?

DOUGLAS. A year. Two years at the most. Just until we
can force more money to continue treatment.

BRODUS. *(Not a question.)* Two years at the most.

DOUGLAS. Just until we get that money for treatment.

BRODUS. *(Considering.)* What was the title of the article re-
porting the Oslo research?

DOUGLAS. *(Rapidly.)* *"Uber das Schicksal der nicht spezifisch
behandelten Luetiker."*

BRODUS. "The Fate of Syphilitics Who Are Not Given Spe-
cific Treatment." That's an unwieldy title.

DOUGLAS. *(Having thought about it previously.)* "A Study of
Untreated Syphilis in the Negro Male." That title's clear, un-
cluttered and to the point.

BRODUS. "The Tuskegee Study of Untreated Syphilis in the

Negro Male"? I want "Tuskegee" in there.

DOUGLAS. *(A guarantee.)* That's what it will be called. The Tuskegee Study.... We'll need new blood work —

EVERS. *(Interrupting, unable to remain silent; quietly trying to separate Brodus from Douglas.)* Dr. Brodus, I promised the men treatment. Now we just going to let 'em go? Just leave 'em with nothing?

BRODUS. *(To quiet her.)* It's not nothing.

EVERS. *(Half to herself.)* It sounds like nothing to me.

DOUGLAS. *(Continuing.)* Nurse Evers, we'll need baseline blood work first. Then the spinal taps.

EVERS. The patients don't know what a spinal tap is, Dr. Douglas. And when they find out it's not treatment, they won't come.

DOUGLAS. Then they can't find out.

EVERS. You explain it to them. That it's for their own best good. Maybe then they'll come.

DOUGLAS. *(Gently.)* Better call the spinal taps something else. This is for the good of the men. You understand that, Nurse Evers? We have nothing else. You understand that, don't you?

EVERS. Dr. Brodus, if we —

BRODUS. The patients must believe that nothing has changed.

EVERS. *(Disbelieving.)* What about contagion?

DOUGLAS. We will only keep patients in the study who have non-contagious syphilis. Any patient found contagious is taken out of the study.

EVERS. *(To Brodus.)* And the arsenic injections? The mercury rubs?

DOUGLAS. *(Gently.)* Use heat liniment.

EVERS. *(Caught in the middle.)* Heat liniment?

BRODUS. *(Gently.)* Nurse Evers ... please.

EVERS. Yes, sir.

DOUGLAS. Nurse Evers, those men need help. Don't they?

EVERS. Of course, they do.

DOUGLAS. Would fifty dollars be of help to those men?

EVERS. Fifty dollars is a lot of money in Macon County,

Dr. Douglas.

DOUGLAS. Would fifty dollars life insurance convince those men to stay with this study?

BRODUS. A decent burial would mean a lot to those men. They're buried in feed sacks by the city dump.

DOUGLAS. As long as this research continues, any study patient that dies for whatever reason receives fifty dollars, for burial. I could fight and get that much money, Nurse Evers, if it would convince those men to stay in the study.

BRODUS. *(Quietly.)* You'll be able to keep nursing those patients and their families and take those men to the hospital free of charge if they get sick and know that they're all signed up, right up front, first in line, when the treatment money comes through.... There's a lot of detours on this road, Nurse Evers. But as long as we're going in the general, forward, direction, we got to keep on traveling, don't you think? *(Privately.)* We have one thread tugging at Washington's money. If that thread breaks, then we have nothing. Really nothing.

EVERS. I'm afraid for those men, Dr. Brodus.

BRODUS. Push past that fear, Nurse Evers.

EVERS. I can't.

BRODUS. We don't have a choice here.

EVERS. Seems not.... First in line?

BRODUS. First in line.

EVERS. *(After a moment.)* All right.

BRODUS. Good.

DOUGLAS. *(A sudden solution.)* "Backshots," Nurse Evers. We don't want to frighten the men. Better call those spinal taps, "backshots." *(Brodus and Douglas purposefully exit, leaving Evers alone. She comes forward to a testimony area.)*

EVERS. You've got to go back, Senator. You've got to appreciate Macon County, Alabama, in 1932, to understand what "caring" meant in those times. You've got to think like we thought then.... You're talking about civil rights. I'm talking about people just trying to stay alive. And some other people trying their best to help them. If you want to walk where I walked, you got to be walking that messy middle ground. *(Lights crossfade to Scene 6. Posters appear advertising free treatment. Evers crosses to Caleb.)*

Scene 6

1932. Outside the Possom Hollow Schoolhouse; morning, two weeks have passed. An examining table and a dressing screen have been set up. Evers, in a white gown, is cleaning and sterilizing instruments and getting records ready for the spinal taps. Caleb, the first patient on the first day of this procedure, stands by the screen in mock defiance.

EVERS. *(Busy, not at all threatened; enjoying the interaction.)* And I said take off your shirt.
CALEB. And I said no.
EVERS. Caleb Humphries, take, off, your, shirt. *(Caleb mimics her.)* This is a serious medical procedure, this backshot, Caleb. Now you got to stop this playing around just 'cause we're in this schoolhouse, and you start acting like this here's a hospital and when I ask you to take your shirt off, I'm asking in a medical not a personal way.
CALEB. *(Matching her gravity.)* Then I'll take it off in a medical way, not a personal way.
EVERS. Caleb Humphries, I'm sorry I'm without a piece of shale from Orange Creek at this moment ... so I could throw it upside your head ... in a medical way. Now get undressed; we got four more patients after you this morning. *(He goes behind the screen and starts taking things off; enjoying himself.)*
CALEB. Everything off?
EVERS. Everything.
CALEB. You goin' to stay around?
EVERS. Usually do.
CALEB. What for?
EVERS. Take notes.
CALEB. Can't Dr. Douglas remember on his own.
EVERS. It goes faster if I'm helping ... *(Clothes are hanging*

over the screen.) Pants now.

CALEB.   What you gonna give me in trade?

EVERS.   *(Still busy working, she takes a gown to him.)* Put this gown on.

CALEB.   Gown? *(Pause.)* This don't got no buttons up front.

EVERS.   That's not the front. You've got it on backwards; turn it around.

CALEB.   Good. *(Pause.)* Now what kind of thing is this; my back's open.

EVERS.   Hold it closed with your hand, Caleb.

CALEB.   Now the front's riding up over my ... riding up too high.

EVERS.   Then just leave it, Caleb. I've been a nurse for eight years. I don't think nothing will be surprising me none. *(Caleb enters; he makes his way to the table. Deliberately not paying him much attention.)* Looks good. Now come on out here and sit on the table with your legs hanging over the side while I'm readying things.

CALEB.   *(Getting on the table.)* What's this gonna be?

EVERS.   I suppose you'd call this, well, a "backshot," Caleb. It's like a shot with a needle *(Touching his lower back.)* down here, at this part of your back, so we can check your spine fluid.

CALEB.   It gonna hurt?

EVERS.   Probably.

CALEB.   You don't do much pretending do you, Nurse Evers?

EVERS.   I want my patients to believe what I'm saying, Caleb. They wouldn't be doing that if I told them it wasn't gonna hurt and then it hurt.

CALEB.   I believe you.

EVERS.   You do?

CALEB.   Of course.

EVERS.   Good.... Come on now, let's get you ready for Dr. Douglas.

CALEB.   I don't like that man much. He talks to me like I'm stupid. He says, "Be there on time." I say, "All right." Then he says, again, "Now you be there on time." And I say,

"I said, all right." Then before I can get out, he says again, "Now you be sure to be there.... On time." They always talking to us like that.

EVERS. Macon's like a foreign country to him, Caleb. He's learning as fast as he can. *(Caleb remains unconvinced.)* Now just sit there, with your hands on your lap and don't be touching back here once I start sterilizing it. *(She puts on a face mask and starts painting rubbing antiseptic solution in a circular motion on his lower back.)*

CALEB. That's cold.

EVERS. Has alcohol and iodine in it.

CALEB. Go easy now.

EVERS. I ain't doing nothing.

CALEB. *(Frightened, seeing the mask for the first time.)* What's that mask about?

EVERS. It's about not breathing on your back when I clean it. Keep your head in that direction. Come on. Stop turning.

CALEB. I want to get a look at you. I figure a look at you is good medicine.

EVERS. Didn't know you were into honey talking, Caleb.

CALEB. Why, Nurse Evers, Mama was always complaining to me: "Boy, you got a diploma in smartness at the mouth."

EVERS. That right?

CALEB. Yes, ma'am.... Too bad she's gone. And my wife. And my child.

EVERS. That's what makes you so angry?

CALEB. I look around this place and all I see is everything and everybody broken down; no one ever getting ahead. Folks around here, they just get scraped and scratched every which way 'til they're all worn down. I'm angry 'cause I want to be using my brain and my mouth instead of my hands and my back.

EVERS. You want to get ahead, you gotta first ask yourself what you do well and then go out and try to use it. You're a "talkin' man" so you have to go out and find a way to use that gift for talking, like a salesman or something.

CALEB. You know I was raised Baptist and I'm thinking that when you're raised Baptist you got a better chance of being a "talkin' man" 'cause if you got a good preacher preaching at you each week, you get a feeling for it.

EVERS.   That's what you had?

CALEB.   Yes, ma'am. Every week. Reverend Banks he was a fine preacher. As far back as I can remember, I can remember his preaching. When I was six years old a big lightning storm touched down by the church. The church members said that the lightning was just plain jealous of the voice of Reverend Banks. Well, an old oak tree was cut down by that lightening and fell on the outhouse behind the church. The next Sunday I climbed up on that oak tree and started taking off on the Reverend to the other children. "Raise out of hell"; "keep you eyes on the Lord"; then I warmed up, didn't care what I was saying anymore: "this here tree has brushed this here outhouse 'cause it smelled; smelled; smelled so bad" ... I'm goin' on like that in the biggest, deepest voice a six year old can put on and the Reverend hear me and my mother hear me and the whole choir that's practicing just inside the church while we kids is playing outside, they hear me too. And I was lashed for the wages of sin. This backshot can't hurt worse than that day. After that, every time we were alone, all those children would be yelling at me "Caleb, Caleb, do the Reverend. Do the Reverend." Now I "do the Reverend" for the fun of it.

EVERS.   You are a talking man.

CALEB.   Think so?

EVERS.   Yes. Yes, I do. (*Douglas enters rapidly, wearing a gown, mask and gloves.*)

DOUGLAS.   Sorry to keep you waiting, Nurse Evers. Good morning, Caleb. Nice to see you. (*Caleb stands. Evers helps Douglas adjust his mask. Douglas is efficient but anxious. He wants things to go well.*) So you're our first patient our first day?

EVERS.   Yes, sir.... Is that good?

DOUGLAS.   (*Reassuring.*) Absolutely. We're fresh, we're rested, we're ready to work. Yes, it's good. Of course it is. Now here's how we do this: You just keep sitting the way you are, Caleb. I'm going to locate that spot between the vertebrae in your lower back and make a small needle puncture. Not much to it really.

CALEB.   Good.

DOUGLAS.   First I'm going to ask you to bend your head over. Good. Now. Just a little further. Good. Very good. Now. Here's the most important part: you're going to have to sit very still. Nurse Evers will help you. Especially once the needle is inside your spinal canal; don't move then or that needle might injure the nerves to your legs.

CALEB.   To my legs?

DOUGLAS.   That's right. You understand?

CALEB.   Of course, I understand.

DOUGLAS.   That's why we don't want you to move.

CALEB.   Don't worry, I'm not movin'.

DOUGLAS.   All right; now, here we go. *(To Evers.)* All set?

CALEB.   Yes, sir.

DOUGLAS.   Caleb?

CALEB.   Yes, sir.

DOUGLAS.   Good. Now, I'll just take that needle Nurse Evers.

CALEB.   Let me see it — it's big ...

DOUGLAS.   Not to worry, Caleb. Only a little part will go in. Just this first little part here at the front.... So. *(Douglas starts to position the needle.)*

CALEB.   What's it made out of?

DOUGLAS.   Gold. It's made out of gold.

CALEB.   Well, that's good.

DOUGLAS.   Yes, it is.... So. Here we go. *(Douglas is standing behind the table focused on Caleb's lower back; each time the needle goes in or comes out, it is searingly painful.)*

CALEB.   *(Controlling the pain.)* Aah. You goin' too far.

DOUGLAS.   I have to try to find the spinal canal. *(Calmly, repositioning the needle.)* I'll be as gentle as I can. Please, just sit still. All right, here we go now. *(Douglas focuses intently; he doesn't want to miss again.)*

CALEB.   *(He resists moving and, trying to ignore the intermittent bursts of pain which occur only when the needle is pushed in, automatically falls into his preaching voice; his anger is stronger than the pain and it is this anger that makes his words clear and reso-*

49

nant, despite the procedure.) Ahhh.... That needle is the work of the devil ... it's sharp and burning and greedy gold in color ... ahhh ... (*A catechism.*) What color was Job? Black. What color was Jeremiah? Black. Who was Moses' wife? An Ethiopian. David said he became like a bottle in the smoke. What's natural? It's as natural to be black as the leopard to be spotted.... Ahhhh ...

DOUGLAS. (*Silence; all stop for a moment.*) What in the world are you saying, Caleb?

CALEB. (*Afraid but not in pain.*) Catechism of the Church of the Living God founded by William Christian in Wrightsville, Arkansas, in 1889.

DOUGLAS. Does it help?

CALEB. It keeps my mind from violence, Dr. Douglas.

DOUGLAS. Then just keep saying it.... One more time now. Hold it. (*Needle in suddenly; the next four lines come at once.*)

EVERS. Dr. Douglas —

DOUGLAS. (*Quieting her.*) Please, Nurse Evers.

CALEB. Ahh; no more, I'm getting off this here table now.

DOUGLAS. (*Alarmed.*) No.

EVERS. (*Taking charge.*) Caleb Humphries don't you move, you hear me; you sit there and don't move; you gotta be a walkin' man, not a cripple man; now you sit there and don't move. Stop moving.

CALEB. Ahhhh.

EVERS. Dr. Douglas —

DOUGLAS. (*Over her, triumphant, relieved.*) Got it. There we go. We're all set. (*Carefully.*) Now I'll just collect some fluid if you will be so kind as to give me the test tube, Nurse Evers.

EVERS. Don't move.

DOUGLAS. (*Douglas puts tube under the needle and collects a small amount of fluid.*) There we are. (*He pulls out the needle. The removal of the needle stings.*)

CALEB. What you doing?

DOUGLAS. Just removing the needle. Well. Now if you don't want a bad headache, Caleb, take my advice and sit here for a while. Just sit right here.

CALEB. Why'd you do that to me?

DOUGLAS. I didn't do anything to you, Caleb. It's not uncommon that the exact entrance to the spinal canal can't be found the first time. Unfortunately, that can cause some pain.
CALEB. Dr. Douglas?
DOUGLAS. Yes, Caleb?
CALEB. Practice.
DOUGLAS. I beg your pardon.
CALEB. I said practice, sir, 'cause you're not gonna have a next patient if you go stickin' them the way you stuck me. How many patients you think'll come here when they find out what you're doin' feel like getting a hot screwdriver twisted in your back?
DOUGLAS. There was nothing wrong with the way I performed that spinal tap ... *(Correcting himself.)* backshot. And if you warn the other patients away from this, you'll be depriving those men of government care.
CALEB. I don't have to warn 'em about nothing, sir. They can hear. They hear it once, they start wonderin'. They hear it twice, and you and Nurse Evers are gonna be out of patients as fast as those men can stampede back home and tell their neighbors about them "spinal taps." That ain't no tap, let me tell you. Not what you're doing.
DOUGLAS. I'll just check this fluid, Nurse Evers.
EVERS. Yes, doctor.
DOUGLAS. Thank you for the advice, Caleb. I'm sorry that hurt so much.
CALEB. Well, maybe you didn't mean it to hurt.
DOUGLAS. No, I didn't. Of course I didn't. I'm just trying to help. *(Douglas exits with the fluid.)*
EVERS. Will you tell the others?
CALEB. Hurts like hell.
EVERS. Dr. Douglas will get better.
CALEB. How? By practicing?
EVERS. That's how you get better.
CALEB. Well, next time you put me at the end of the line.... You think I should?
EVERS. What?
CALEB. Tell the others.

EVERS.   You're looking for something that I can't answer for you, Caleb.

CALEB.   Why not?

EVERS.   I'm a nurse. I'm here to help Dr. Douglas get done what needs to be done. That's my job.

CALEB.   We need to be healthy. That's what needs to be done. Right?

EVERS.   Yes.

CALEB.   I'm just asking you, if this is making me healthy? *(Evers is preparing for the next patient. Caleb watches her for a few moments.)* See, Nurse Evers, I don't trust the white. You gotta watch them. So they don't be sneaking up on you. No white folks with money come around when my wife took ill or my baby was born sick.

EVERS.   Hanging onto that anger won't help you win, Caleb.

CALEB.   *(Evers is cleaning the wound. It stings.)* Nurse Evers, I gotta keep angry to work my place, to save my money ... sometimes just to get up in the morning.

EVERS.   I can understand that.

CALEB.   You can? You don't seem like a get-up-in-the-mornin'-angry to me.

EVERS.   I'm not. I'm more the go-to-sleep-angry kind.

CALEB.   I can't seem to do that. Can't get to sleep when I'm angry.

EVERS.   You must be up a lot of nights.

CALEB.   I am. Yes, I am.

EVERS.   Got to trust somebody, Caleb.

CALEB.   Maybe.

EVERS.   Sometime. How else you going to live? No one can make it just on their own.

CALEB.   *(Pause.)* You been a good friend to people around here.

EVERS.   They're my family.

CALEB.   You never been married?

EVERS.   Too busy.

CALEB.   Getting an education. Getting trained as a nurse so you can polish silver.

EVERS.   Now there's some anger that I went to sleep with

a few nights. But I was patient. Now here I am doing what I was trained to do.... And I got a job offer. A nursing job. In New York City.

CALEB. You taking it?

EVERS. Thinking about it. I've started thinking seriously about it.

CALEB. I'd take it if I was you.

EVERS. You would?

CALEB. In a minute. And take me with you.

EVERS. What about the gilleein'?

CALEB. Take them too. We'll hire a bus. Dance up in Harlem.... You got a first name?

EVERS. Yes.

CALEB. You gonna tell me what it is?

EVERS. Why you want to know?

CALEB. When I talk about this saintly woman with God's gift of beauty and compassion, it's gonna lose something if I can't make a direct connection by using your first name.

EVERS. When you going to be doing that kind of talking?

CALEB. To myself. When I need the company of a woman I respect.

EVERS. It's unusual.

CALEB. Lorraine?

EVERS. No.

CALEB. Madelaine?

EVERS. No.

CALEB. Sally Ann?

EVERS. Eunice.

CALEB. That's a fine name. Sounds like it got "nice" in it, don't it?

EVERS. You can God-taik and sweet-talk, can't you, Caleb?

CALEB. I don't have to be pepper all the time. And you don't have to be alone all the time neither.

EVERS. I got the work.

CALEB. That ain't a person.

EVERS. No. But it's my life. The work with you all is my life. *(They look at each other for a moment.)*

CALEB. No time for specials ... Eunice?

EVERS.   *(Struggling.)* No, Caleb. No time. I got to treat all my patients the same.

CALEB.   *(Direct.)* I'll be putting my trust in you. If you don't mind.

EVERS.   *(Troubled.)* Caleb ...

CALEB.   If you don't mind ...

EVERS.   *(Recovering.)* Well. Sure. I don't mind. Of course, I don't. *(Trying to end the conversation with a smile.)* I've never seen no patient, ever, preach gospel through it all.

CALEB.   I told you. It just comes on out. Natural like.

EVERS.   Well, you take off that gown, "talkin' man."

CALEB.   You meanin' that in a medical way or a personal way?

EVERS.   And then get dressed ... behind the screen. *(She continues preparing for the next patient. As Caleb crosses behind the screen, he looks over his shoulder and starts singing "Children, Don't Be Afraid"* to Evers, a modest, simple serenade. After a while, Evers crosses to Dr. Brodus' office with the spinal tap data as the lights fade.)*

Scene 7

1932. Dr. Brodus' office. Three days later. Evers enters delivering the spinal tap reports to Brodus.

EVERS.   Painful to watch. Every one of them. Very painful.

BRODUS.   Looks like he got the fluid. *(Brodus begins to tabulate the results of the spinal taps.)*

EVERS.   "It won't hurt but a little. It's so important to your health." I couldn't stand the pain. But the lying don't suit me much either, Dr. Brodus.

BRODUS.   You don't tell a man he's going to die or go

---

* See Special Note on Songs and Recordings on copyright page.

blind. You soften it. The patients know we're zigzagging 'round the truth once in a while. That's part of being humane.

EVERS.   You tell a man a "backshot" is helping him ... feels like lying. *(Controlled.)* Dr. Brodus, I'm giving these men back rubs with heat liniment and calling it "mercury."

BRODUS.   You've got to step back. You've got to look from a distance.

EVERS.   I can't. I'm up close. You're doing the research. I'm doing the "zigzagging."

BRODUS.   We're committed now. You'll just have to do without the luxury of feeling safely upright when a whole people is dying.

EVERS.   I just want to tell the men what's going on. The straight truth. "There's no mercury in those back rubs. They won't stop bad blood. But you got to stick with it so when new money comes you'll be right up front, first in line..." The straight truth.

BRODUS.   No. They wouldn't understand and then they'd be lost to treatment when new money does come through.

EVERS.   Dr. Brodus, this just don't sit well with me.... Now I appreciate everything you've done. Everything you're doing for me. For all of us ...

BRODUS.   And?

EVERS.   I've been offered a position. In New York City. Night supervisor.

BRODUS.   I see.

EVERS.   I'm thinking about taking it.

BRODUS.   Is that what you learned here? To run when the fire gets hot? You're needed here. To those men there's only one nurse. You leave and the next time we go around to find those men, they won't be there.... You go to New York, you're going for yourself.

EVERS.   I love those men.

BRODUS.   Then stay with them. Stay with them. And carry your burden yourself. Don't ask those men to carry it.

EVERS.   I'm a nurse. I'm not a scientist.

BRODUS.   There is no difference. Not here. Not now. Not

for us.

EVERS.   Feels to me like there is. Feels to me like there surely is. *(Lights crossfade for Scene 8 as Willie and Ben enter and Brodus exits. Evers remains, watching.)*

Scene 8

1932. Inside the Possom Hollow Schoolhouse. One week later. The evening of a gillee competition. Ben is looking at the blackboard. Willie enters carrying a small, wooden staircase consisting of three steps. He begins practicing his gillee performance. Evers watches, troubled.

WILLIE.   Ben Washington, you ready?... *(Practicing.)* One, two, buck, tap, drop, tap.

BEN.   Ready as I'll ever be.

WILLIE.   'Cause Miss Ever's Lodge and Burial Society is cruising into Macon in our government limousine to win us a plow. *(Referring to the stairs.)* Nurse Evers, you know which way this secret staircase is heading.

EVERS.   *(Distracted.)* Which way, Willie?

WILLIE.   North.

EVERS.   Amen to that.

WILLIE.   *(Calling outside the schoolhouse.)* Hodman. Caleb. The gilleein' fixin' to start without us. *(To Evers and Ben.)* I'm going to keep an eye out for them. I'll give a horn and a shout soon as they come. *(Willie exits, calling.)* Caleb. Hodman.

BEN.   *(Looking at the blackboard.)* Miss Evers?

EVERS.   Yes, Ben.

BEN.   You're a nurse. You know things.

EVERS.   Some things.

BEN.   I was wondering. "Ben" is a short name. Just three letters, right?

EVERS.   Right.

BEN.   How would you write it?

EVERS.   Like this. *(She writes in script on the board.)* "Ben."

BEN. *Slower.* So I could see how you do it. Maybe I could draw it myself.

EVERS. The first letter is a "B." *(She writes block letters, one at a time.)*

BEN. Like two hills turned on their side.

EVERS. Yes. Like two hills turned on their side. *(Continuing.)* Then this is an "E." *(She realizes how to teach him.)* Like a main street with three streets leaving, all in the same direction.

BEN. All right.

EVERS. And this is an "N." ... Let's see ...

BEN. *(He takes the chalk.)* Here. Like two sides of a road with a man walking from one end across to the other end.

EVERS. Yes, sir, it is.

BEN. *(He draws his name.)* "Two hills on their side; main street and three dead ends; a man crossing from one side of the road to the other." That's my name.

EVERS. "Ben."

BEN. Part of it, anyway. I don't think I have living time left to learn "Washington." Do you?

EVERS. I think you could.

BEN. I'm 57 years old, you know. And no one but you ever took the time to learn me how to write. It ain't that hard.

EVERS. You're a quick student, Ben.

BEN. I'm depending on you ... for the "Washington" part. Then a word or two more. Then two or three more ... I got Aspiration, don't I?

EVERS. Without a doubt, Ben Washington.

BEN. You going to have the time to teach them words to me, Nurse Evers?

EVERS. I'm leaving Monday week, Ben.

BEN. So I hear.

EVERS. You angry?

BEN. You're an important person here, Nurse Evers.

EVERS. Not me. Come on. The doctors and lawyers and such, they're the important ones. Lord, not me.

BEN. You're important to the ones that don't have the money to talk to all those doctors and lawyers. But you're a humble person so you don't see that. I just wanted you to

57

know how it is, while you can still cash in that train ticket.

EVERS.   Ben, there are some things that you just can't keep doing because if you do them, you know you going to become twisted in your mind.

BEN.   What kind of things you talking about?

EVERS.   Things that you got to carry yourself when you're a nurse. Private kinds of things.

BEN.   "Leaves of sorrow," that's how my wife used to call those private things. Sorrowful leaves dropping one by one to the ground every winter.... Nurse Evers, there ain't nothing that you could do, nothing, that could make it worse than what we already got. You a religious woman, Nurse Evers?

EVERS.   You know I am.

BEN.   Yes, I do. You got to trust that God will untwist your mind. (Car honk. Willie appears at the door.)

WILLIE.   Come on. They're here. Let's go. We're losing gasoline. (Willie exits.)

BEN.   Nurse Evers, we're going to drown without you reaching out for us, holding our heads above the water. We're going to just plain drown. (Car honk. Light change. Willie re-enters, carrying his staircase. He is accompanied by Hodman and Caleb. We are now outside the schoolhouse. During the following dialogue the car is constructed by the men using boxes of various sizes. The vehicle is not realistic and has two levels: a front seat carrying Miss Evers, the driver, and Caleb; and a back, elevated area holding Hodman, Ben, and Willie. This vehicle will soon be transformed by the men into the gillee stage. There is a small American flag and a larger government seal somewhere in evidence. Miss Evers' Boys are high, almost frenetic in anticipation. During the ride, the men tap out rhythms, and sing snatches of melody or harmony with the distant Victrola record sound, a sound that grows and is layered as the scene progresses.)

CALEB.   Let's go. (They are all building the car.)

HODMAN.   Yes, sir. Miss Evers' Boys is on their way to glory. (Music. Light change as Evers begins to drive. She is thoughtful.)

WILLIE.   Let's go past Totes' House on the Public Road.

HODMAN.   There's Dan Madge's place.

BEN.   Too bad he's gone.

WILLIE. Nice funeral.

BEN. Very nice.

HODMAN. Well, that's something. Dan Madge. He had that government insurance, didn't he, Nurse Evers? Like we got?

EVERS. Yes, he did.

HODMAN. That's what helped that family I can tell you that. He wouldn't have had nothing but a made-at-home box without that money.

WILLIE. Nothing more important —

OTHER MEN. (Laughing, teasing Willie by talking along with him.) — than life insurance.

HODMAN. We got it by heart, Willie.

WILLIE. Well, it's true.... Sent him up to Tuskegee first.

HODMAN. What for?

WILLIE. You tell me. Why should they be wanting to send you to the hospital after you're dead? What can they do for you?

CALEB. Nothing.

WILLIE. I asked Kirk up by the main house.

CALEB. What he say?

WILLIE. Say: "What you askin' a white man for?" I told him I thought he might know. He just look away and spit.

EVERS. He did that?

WILLIE. Through that ugly hole between his two front teeth. Then I asked Dan's wife, Sheila.

CALEB. What she say?

WILLIE. Said the school up there wanted to take a look at him.

HODMAN. Hell, he was ugly before he died.

CALEB. White folks get sent to the hospital before you're dead; colored, after.

HODMAN. Amen.... (They travel.) Willie, last time you was checked, did your doctor ask you to get in your "birthday suit"?

WILLIE. No, sir. just told me to strip.

HODMAN. That what that means? He say, "Get in your birthday suit." Then he leaves the room. He comes back and says, "Why aren't you in your birthday suit." I don't know what this man's taking about. What kind of way is that for a doctor to talk, Nurse Evers? "Birthday suit."

EVERS.   He didn't want to offend you, Hodman.

WILLIE.   By telling you to "strip naked."

HODMAN.   Why he want me strip naked anyway?

EVERS.   So he can examine you.

HODMAN.   He can examine me without having me strip naked.

BEN.   That doctor got to snoop around your corners, Hodman.

WILLIE.   "Snoop around yo' corners." *(Evers begins to enjoy this banter in spite of the burden she carries.)*

HODMAN.   Don't got no corners. I'm all straight and pointy right out to the horizon.

WILLIE.   Whooeee.

CALEB.   What you been nipping, Hodman?

HODMAN.   We're all men here tonight aren't we, Nurse Evers?

EVERS.   Seems so.

WILLIE.   *(Looking at the unseen Tote as they drive by.)* Hey, Tote. We'll be driving back later on this way, one plow richer. See if we don't. So long, Tote. Keep swatting those flies and feeding them to your chicken.

EVERS.   *(After a moment.)* You boys got to win tonight.

BEN.   Why? 'Cause you're leaving?

EVERS.   No, not because I'm leaving.

HODMAN.   Because I'm pointy right out to the horizon?

EVERS.   Even if you were, Hodman, you wouldn't win nothing for it. *(The men enjoy her response.)* Because you're the best. That's when you deserve to win. When you're the best.

BEN.   Yes, sir.

WILLIE.   I am and we are.

HODMAN.   We ain't going to change our name, Nurse Evers. Been good luck for us. That suit you?

EVERS.   Sure.

CALEB.   Miss Evers' Lodge is going to dance for glory. *(The car stops. They've arrived.)* Willie, you going to start off "turtle style?"

WILLIE.   No, sir. Jackspring. Like this. *(Drums a rhythm; the others start to join and build on the rhythm.)* Then a little bucking and some trail-alongs.

HODMAN.   And a jump —

WILLIE.   Three jumps. *(He jumps out of the car; the others follow.)*

CALEB.   That's it.

BEN.   No mercy.

WILLIE.   Do the Reverend, Caleb. Do the Reverend. *(They begin to change the car into the flatback of a truck — the gillee stage. As the men create the gillee, Caleb fires them up by imitating Reverend Banks, a ritual that they have participated in before. Rhythmic sounds growing in volume can be heard behind him. Evers watchers them with admiration.)*

CALEB.   Ezekiel was in the valley of the dry bones.... Oh ye dried bones —

OTHER MEN.   *(Answering variously.)* Yes, sir — Amen — yeah — tell it — Mmmmmmm —

CALEB.   Hear the word, the word of the Lord.

OTHER MEN.   *(Answering.)* Yes, sir — Amen — yeah — tell it — Mmmmmmm —

CALEB.   Can these bones live? God make the bones in man.

OTHER MEN.   Yes, sir — Amen — yeah — tell it — Mmmmmmm —

CALEB.   I can't hear you, Nurse Evers. *(Throughout the following Evers is increasingly drawn into the magic of the gospel.)* God make the blood in man.

EVERS/OTHER MEN.   Yes, sir — Amen — yeah — tell it — Mmm-mmmm —

CALEB.   What you say, Nurse Evers? God make the spirit in man.

EVERS/OTHER MEN.   Yes, sir — Amen — yeah — tell it — Mmmmmmm —

CALEB, MEN and EVERS.
Spirit make the blood flow/ **YES SIR**
Blood make the muscle hot/ **YES SIR**
Muscle make the bones move/ **YES SIR**
Bones make the spirit dance/ **YES SIR**

Bones came together ...

EVERS. *(Momentary freeze; as testimony, simple and quiet.)* The night of that gillee, I decided to stay in Macon County.

MEN/EVERS. *(Answering Caleb's last Reverend line with a shout.)* AMEN. *(Car lights suddenly spotlight the men. The performance springs to life with spirited, sharp, desperate sound and movement. A crude banner identifying "Miss Evers' Boys" appears. The men use the following as part of their gillee performance responding with "YEAH" after each phrase with increasing intensity. It is an authentic, winning performance.)*

CALEB/MEN.

Head bone, head bone in the neck bone/ YEAH

Neck bone, neck bone in the shoulder bone/ YEAH

Shoulder bone, shoulder bone in the rib bone/ YEAH

Rib bone, rib bone in the back bone/ YEAH

Back bone, back bone in the hip bone/ YEAH

Hip bone, hip bone in the thigh bone/ YEAH

Thigh bone, thigh bone in the leg bone/ YEAH

Leg bone, leg bone in the ankle bone/ YEAH

Ankle bone, ankle bone in the foot bone/ YEAH

(The rhythm becomes increasingly frenzied as Willie dances to it. Evers watches with admiration as the gillee music grows and is amplified. At the same time light surrounds the men in a confining, microscopic circle, burning bright. Another light reveals Evers. The circular seal of the United States Public Health Service appears. Sudden stillness and the fading echo of a Victrola record. Light intensifies on Evers as she turns and stares at the audience. Lights fade to black.)

END OF ACT ONE

ACT TWO

Scene 1

1946. Simultaneously, three separate playing areas appear. On one part of the Stage, Willie in a pool of dim downlight is quietly testing his legs by practicing his dance turns again and again to perfection. Caleb, Hodman, and Ben holding their instruments stand in the shadows, watching Willie. The play of light and shadow is not realistic.

On another part of the stage Brodus and Douglas are dimly revealed surveying slides using two microscopes in Brodus' office. By turns they enter plot points on a large graph they have created on a blackboard. The work is quiet and methodical. This setting and activity will continue throughout the treatment center scene until interrupted by Willie's arrival in Brodus' office.

Evers stands between these two settings downstage center.

WILLIE.   *(A private whisper, as he practices.)* Da, da, da ... da, da.

EVERS.   *(As testimony.)* When you're up close for fourteen years, you don't notice the changes.... Unless they catch you by surprise. But even then, after a while, those surprises get familiar and it almost seems like nothing has changed.... Those men looked healthy. No pain or nothing like that. And they felt good. You wouldn't believe anything was wrong with them. That's the kind of disease it was, see. Hidden. Some people in this room might have syphilis at this very moment and you wouldn't know it. No offense meant, Senator.

I'm not saying there weren't consequences. I'm just saying it wasn't that simple. The disease was not predictable. And there was no money. And the treatment was dangerous.

63

Convulsions. And teeth would fall out. It was ridiculous. I came to believe that if a person looked good, you best just leave them be.

But 1946 changed all that. Something new arrived, something that changed everything. The "silver bullet," they called it: penicillin. Meningitis, cured. Pneumonia, cured. Finally. And now, syphilis, cured. A national treatment program. And my patients were going to be first in line.

(Day 1.)

BRODUS.   *(Lights up; looking up from his work.)* That's not possible. *(Evers turns to Douglas and Brodus.)*
EVERS.   First in line. That's what we said. That's what you told me. That was the promise.
DOUGLAS.   *(Reasonable.)* First we must stop the disease from spreading. Contagious patients first. *(Brodus and Douglas continue to plot graph numbers on a large blackboard.)*

(Day 2.)

(Lights up; Willie suddenly stops dancing and grabs his legs.)

WILLIE.   Help. Help. *(Lights change. Evers moves to him, alarmed. Evers is fearful that it is syphilis that is starting to cripple Willie but she is uncertain as to diagnosis and desperately seeks hope in that uncertainty. The men and Evers gather around Willie.)* I'm sorry I yelled like that. I couldn't see what I was doing my eyes were watering so bad.... Like a baby. Yelling.
EVERS.   *(Cradling Willie.)* You were in pain. It's OK to yell, Willie. *(She rolls up his pants legs.)* I'm losing it. I'm spooked.
CALEB.   Don't say that.
HODMAN.   You the star attraction, Willie.
BEN.   You lose it. We lose it too.
EVERS.   Rest, Willie. Let me look after that leg for you. *(She begins to massage his legs.)*

WILLIE.   Dad. Real bad. I'm losing it all.

EVERS.   *(Determined.)* No, you're not. You'll be all right, Willie. You're not going to lose it all. You can't be thinking like that. Come on now. Let's work on this leg. *(The men quietly attend to Willie. Evers speaks to Brodus and Douglas, determined. The men do not hear her. She continues to work on Willie until the argument pulls her to Brodus and Douglas.)*

(Day 3.)

EVERS.   *(To Brodus and Douglas.)* Willie's beginning to drag his leg.

BRODUS.   Who?

EVERS.   Willie Johnson. I don't know what's wrong with him ...

BRODUS.   And?

EVERS.   I want to know what's wrong with him. I want to bring him here. To be examined. By both you gentlemen.

BRODUS.   Why?

EVERS.   Dr. Brodus, he's one of the study patients.

BRODUS.   I see.... Bring him.

EVERS.   I will. I sure will.

(Day 4.)

(Evers is suddenly pulled into the men's scene by Willie's cry and Caleb's command.)

WILLIE.   *(In pain.)* Ahhhh.

CALEB.   *(Angry.)* You need some doctorin', boy.

EVERS.   *(Stung.)* He got some.

CALEB.   Well, it ain't doing him no good.

BEN.   What you mad at her for?

HODMAN.   Caleb —

CALEB.   These legs are walking out of here for all of us. Without Willie, we're nothing.

EVERS.   I'll speak to Dr. Douglas.

CALEB.   I'm not talking about more back rubs. I'm talking about something different. Something new. For his leg.

EVERS.   I said I'll speak to Dr. Douglas when he comes down next week. And I've already spoken to Dr. Brodus. I'll get them both to examine you, Willie. Personally. To see what's bothering you. For right now you need some of those pink aspirin pills, that's for sure. But you got to know exactly what's bothering you before you can treat it permanent, see? You got to give it a name: like arthritis, or rheumatism, or gout, or just plain too much hard work. You got to name it before you can fix it, see? Now you're under my care, Willie. I've watched after you all these years. Haven't I? And your wife, Hodman? And your niece, Caleb? Ben? You all have been doing all right, haven't you?

CALEB.   *(Sharply.)* We gotta get these feet moving right, Nurse Evers. Now.

EVERS.   I know, Caleb. I know.

BEN.   What you fussin' at her for? What's wrong with you?

CALEB.   Don't nobody do nothing for you. You gotta do it for yourself. Willie, you gotta get some new doctorin'.

EVERS.   No, Caleb.

WILLIE.   Can't afford it.

CALEB.   You gotta afford it. Ain't nothing more important to you than your legs. Sell that heifer you got.

WILLIE.   *(Willie works on his legs.)* I'm waiting. Waiting for the Lord to put his hands on my shoulders.

CALEB.   *(Sharply.)* No, Willie. You don't have no waiting time left. None of us do. Now stop thinking and start movin'. You're not rich enough to feel sorry for yourself. Come on. Get moving. "Gotta work." Come on.

HODMAN.   Willie, drink you a quart of May tea at the beginning of the month.

CALEB.   What are you selling him?

HODMAN.   I seen it work. You see what I'm saying to you, Willie?

WILLIE.   All I see is grandpa laying in the dirt.

CALEB.   You got dying on the brain, Willie Johnson.

WILLIE. It preys on my mind, Caleb.

BEN. It don't have to. We got our own burial society. That's right, ain't it, Nurse Evers?

EVERS. Yes, Ben. That's right.

CALEB. If you're dead it don't matter what they do to you.

EVERS. Got your Aspiration, don't you, Willie?

WILLIE. That Aspiration ain't won nothing in seven months.

CALEB. Come on. You got to work that pain out of those legs.

EVERS. That's it, Willie. That's what you got to do. *(Willie begins to stand up. Evers is now caught between the two scenes.)*

(Day 5.)

EVERS. Dr. Brodus, my patients have waited the longest. They need penicillin the most. It would help them.

BRODUS. Penicillin can't undo the damage that has already been done.

EVERS. It might stop them from getting worse.

BRODUS. Perhaps. Or it might kill them.

EVERS. *(Stands.)* Penicillin?

BRODUS. The Herxheimer reaction.

EVERS. *(Crossing to Douglas and Brodus.)* Herxheimer?

BRODUS. An allergic reaction that could kill a chronic syphilitic with a single injection of penicillin.

EVERS. Like the arsenic?

BRODUS. Worse.

DOUGLAS. Washington is researching the question now. To determine the degree of risk.

(Day 6.)

(Willie is standing, holding his legs.)

CALEB. Gotta work.

EVERS. *(To Willie.)* Come on, Willie. You got your Aspira-

67

tion, don't you?

WILLIE. Yes, ma'am. Nothing's going to beat me out of my ticket to the Cotton Club. *(Willie tentatively tests his legs.)*

EVERS. *(To Brodus and Douglas.)* And if there's no risk, then he'll get the penicillin. Right?

CALEB. Do that one again, Willie.

EVERS. Don't look down, Willie. Look straight out and dance through the pain.... *(To Brodus and Douglas.)* How long until Washington decides the risk?

DOUGLAS. You can't hurry this kind of investigation. It's too dangerous. You make mistakes.

CALEB. "Gotta work."

EVERS. Come on, Willie. *(Hoping.)* There's nothing wrong with that leg.

HODMAN. Willie, do like you always do.

EVERS. Dance that pain down, Willie.

HODMAN. Come on, Willie. Gotta work.

CALEB. Gotta work.

EVERS. *(To Brodus and Douglas.)* How long? Exactly how long are they going to have to wait?

BRODUS. As soon as there's a decision to do so, we'll move to treat every patient in the study.

MEN. Gotta work ... gotta work. *(Quietly but insistently the men use their instruments and the phrase "gotta work" to create a rhythm to push Willie to dance. The words become embedded in a combination of vocal sounds and driving hand and foot percussion. There is desperation in this crusade. The sounds are sharp and tinged with anger. Willie forces himself to dance through the pain. The pain is always there but the determination to ignore it grows during the following lines. This combination of word and sound underscores the following dialogue.)*

EVERS. Got to fight it, Willie. Got to fight it hard ...

WILLIE. *(Determined.)* Gotta work, gotta work ...

EVERS. *(To Brodus and Douglas.)* These men need all the help they can get. Right now.

DOUGLAS. Right now, you better look after those men. If the spirochete is embedded in the heart muscle and penicillin kills the germ, holes could be left in that muscle and the heart might disintegrate —

EVERS. What?

WILLIE.. *(Willie dances past the pain and shouts, triumphant.)* You hear me, Grandpa. I'm gonna win 'cause I'm going to do that double fly step, the one you taught me, you hear.

EVERS. What? *(A cry.)* Dr. Brodus?

BRODUS. The heart might explode. *(Light change.)*

EVERS. *(Turning into the new scene; a frightened shout.)* There's two men in this treatment center who have no place being here. *(Lights crossfade to Scene 2 as Evers moves to the rapid treatment center and Brodus and Douglas continue working. Hodman and Ben exit. Willie and Caleb move into the next scene.)*

Scene 2

1946. A Birmingham rapid treatment center. One month later. The setting is defined by two benches. Caleb and Willie are waiting in line behind one bench. Evers is standing on another bench. In the background, Douglas and Brodus continue smoothly plotting points on the graph.

EVERS. *(Continuing as the setting changes around her.)* Is there a patient here named, Willie Johnson? Is there a patient in this treatment center named Caleb Humphries?

WILLIE. *(Willie stands on the bench and yells to Evers across the room.)* Yes. I'm here. Over here. Behind you, Nurse Evers. *(She turns to him.)* You're wearing a new hat.

EVERS. *(Yelling.)* What you doin' here, Willie Johnson?

CALEB. *(Caleb stands on the bench next to Willie.)* We're here to get a hip shot of that penicillin, Nurse Evers.

EVERS. No sir. No sir, you're not. You're government patients. You're not supposed to be here. Now come on over here so we're not disturbing all these people. *(The men and Evers come together.)*

WILLIE. The doctor sent us to come.

EVERS. What doctor? That doctor didn't know you were a

United States Government patient. If that doctor knew that, he wouldn't have sent you. Now you get on that bus and go on back to Tuskegee. Penicillin ain't for you. And what are you doing here, Caleb?

CALEB.   Sam Heart's brother's here. He's getting a shot. Tom Daniel's cousin's here. He's getting it. I talked to those men. You know what they got?

EVERS.   What?

CALEB.   Bad blood. That's what I got, ain't it? They're getting a hip shot of that penicillin. That's what I'm getting. And Willie.

EVERS.   No. You're not.

CALEB.   Yes. I am.

EVERS.   Caleb. That shot could kill you.

CALEB.   They're all still standing. Over there in the other room.

EVERS.   They're different from both of you.

CALEB.   They got bad blood. Just like us.

EVERS.   No. It's different. They just got it. You all had it for years. They're not in danger from this penicillin. You all are. It could make holes in you heart. Make it explode. And there's nothing bothering you, Caleb.

CALEB.   Nothing. Now.

EVERS.   That's right. Nothing. And, Willie, this is not the kind of chance you want to take.

CALEB.   We don't see it like that.

EVERS.   Well, I do. *(To Willie.)* You know what penicillin is?

WILLIE.   Some kind of medicine.

EVERS.   It's a mold.

WILLIE.   A mold?

EVERS.   Like you find under a tree.... It's a mold.

WILLIE.   And it can kill you, you say?

EVERS.   We don't know. That's why we have to wait. Until we're certain it's safe. Please. We got to wait.

CALEB.   I'm not waiting.

EVERS.   You're a government patient.

CALEB.   I don't want to be no government patient no more.

EVERS.   And you won't be if you get that shot. If you live.

WILLIE.   Mold ain't goin' to be doin' me much good, I don't guess.

EVERS.   We ain't givin' you no mold in Macon County. Come on. *(Willie moves to leave with Evers.)*

CALEB.   You stay right here, Willie.

WILLIE.   What's wrong with you? You heard what she said.

CALEB.   I don't trust the government.

WILLIE.   I'm not talking to the government, Caleb. I'm talking to Nurse Evers. *(Evers and Willie start to leave.)* Come on, Caleb. Let's go. That stuff no good for us.

EVERS.   I'll tell them not to give you that shot.

CALEB.   You do that. I'll get it somewhere else.

EVERS.   I'm worried for you, Caleb. Please.

CALEB.   No. That may be the only word I have left to me, Nurse Evers. But I can still use it.... No. *(He sits.)*

EVERS.   Come on, Willie.

CALEB.   *(Desperate, calling after him.)* Willie ... Willie ... *(Evers escorts Willie to Dr. Brodus' office as lights crossfade and Caleb exits.)*

Scene 3

Dr. Brodus' office. One week later. Evers escorts Willie to Brodus. Douglas concludes a calculation at the blackboard.

EVERS.   *(Escorting him from the treatment center.)* Come on, Willie ... *(Now into the new scene.)* Come on, come on in.... Willie Johnson, this is Dr. Brodus.

WILLIE.   Never thought I'd be standing in your office, Dr. Brodus.

BRODUS.   Well, don't. Sit down. No not there. Sit here. Good. Now take off your shoes. Roll up your pants. Let's take a look at you.

DOUGLAS.   *(Coming forward, cordial.)* Hello, Willie Johnson.

WILLIE.   Dr. Douglas in town? Must be spring examination time.

DOUGLAS.   Nice to see you again, Willie.

71

WILLIE.   You here to examine me, too?

DOUGLAS.   If you don't mind.

WILLIE.   Mind? No, sir. Looks like I'm riding in the front of the train for this one, ain't I?

BRODUS.   Willie, what's the problem?

WILLIE.   Nurse Evers tell you about my leg?

BRODUS.   Yes.

WILLIE.   That's the problem.

BRODUS.   *(Brodus goes to examine Willie.)* Willie, pull your toes up while I try to push them down. *(Brodus puts one hand on top of Willie's left foot and one hand under Willie's heel. He pushes the toes down as Willie is trying to pull them up.)* Strong. That's good. Now the other foot. *(He tests that foot. It is not as strong.)* Good. Now stand, please. *(Willie does so.)* Put your feet together and close your eyes. *(Willie does so. They watch to see if he will fall. He doesn't.)* Good. Now put one foot up on the other knee and balance. *(Willie does so. All these tests are normal.)* Good. Now walk. *(Willie starts to walk.)* No. One foot in front of the other. Toe to heel. *(Willie walks pass the doctors with one foot directly in front of the other. The right foot drags slightly. To Douglas, quietly but proving a point.)* Look. Right there, Dr. Douglas. The right foot. *(Willie suddenly turns back.)*

WILLIE.   What you saying?

EVERS.   Doctor talk, Willie.

BRODUS.   Just keep walking, Mr. Johnson. *(Willie does so.)* See there. *(A warning.)* How he's beginning to drag his right foot.

DOUGLAS.   Yes, I see it.

BRODUS.   Now try something more difficult.

EVERS.   Do some gilleein' for them, Willie.

BRODUS.   *(Brodus watches intently.)* You see, Dr. Douglas. *(Accusing.)* The slight slurring of that right foot.

DOUGLAS.   I can see it, Dr. Brodus.

BRODUS.   And watch. He'll look down every few seconds — just keep dancing, Mr. Johnson — to check on his foot. *(They watch.)*

DOUGLAS.   All right, Willie. You can stop now. *(Willie stops.)*

BRODUS.   You did very well.

WILLIE.   How well?

BRODUS. Why don't you go next door, rest, then come on back in and we'll talk some more.

WILLIE. Look good though?

BRODUS. You're a fine dancer, Willie.

WILLIE. Gilleein'. It's called gilleein', Dr. Brodus. *(Willie exits.)*

EVERS. He's been healthy up to now, Dr. Brodus. Real healthy. And strong. And Willie works very hard. With horses. Sometimes the men get kicked or stepped on and they don't pay it no mind because they can't stop working and —

BRODUS. No. I don't think so.

EVERS. You're sure?

BRODUS. Yes.

EVERS. After all these years of nothing?

BRODUS. Yes.

EVERS. I see. Well, what we going to do? Time's running out here.

DOUGLAS. Nurse Evers, I appreciate your attachment to Willie. To all your patients. But unless we proceed in a professional manner we could be doing a greater harm.

EVERS. See what we got to do, Dr. Douglas, is explain that Herxheimer risk to Mr. Johnson and let him choose. I think at this point he'd choose to be treated.

DOUGLAS. He very well might do that. We've all seen patients who are so desperate that they would choose to take any treatment regardless of the consequences. Because they can't be objective. They don't have the understanding —

EVERS. *(Interrupting.)* Then let's give them that understanding. Maybe they don't want to take that Herxheimer risk. Maybe they do.

DOUGLAS. Herxheimer is no longer my concern. Washington's assessment is that penicillin is only a small risk to these late-stage syphilitics.

EVERS. Penicillin's all right? Well, that's good news. Fine news. God knows Willie needs all the help he can get.

DOUGLAS. I didn't say penicillin's all right. I said it was only a small risk to Willie. But Willie's not my concern right now. I'm concerned for the thousands of contagious, untreated syphilitics all over the county.

EVERS. How's that?

DOUGLAS. We are part of a national treatment program. We must treat six-thousand contagious patients, not in the study, with penicillin, right here in Macon County. Some of those patients are suspicious, fearful of new medicine and they all know Willie's a government patient. So if we give Willie penicillin and he dies, contagious patients with far less risk, patients who could be helped by penicillin, might refuse to be treated with it. And then the disease lives on and continues to spread.... I'm not willing to jeopardize that work. And I don't think you are either.... I'll go get Willie. We must wait until the treatment program is less vulnerable. We must wait. *(Douglas exits to get Willie. Brodus and Evers are left alone. They do not speak. For a few moments they wait in silence.)*

EVERS. Whoosh-Shuffle. Slap, slap shuffle.... Soon I'll know it's Willie just by hearing how he walks up to the clinic door. The Slapwalk Shuffle in those old syphilitics. Old being forty-five....

BRODUS. *(After a moment.)* I once did two autopsies at the same time. On two patients, both in their thirties. Laid out next to each other. I took out their hearts and put them on a scale and weighed them both. Together. Then I went about some other business. When I came back I realized I hadn't tagged those hearts. I didn't know which one came from which patient. Now that was more than embarrassing. You see there was a white man laid out on one table and a colored man on the other. Now if I put the white heart in the colored patient.... Or the colored heart in the white patient.... So I looked at those two hearts for a long time. I held both of them up in my hands examining them. For the longest time.... Then I closed my eyes and put a heart in each body and sewed them up. As simple as that.... Nurse Evers, we got a chance to do something special right now. To push people past the hate, past the idea of difference. Don't you think that's what we got to do?

EVERS. *(Not convinced.)* Penicillin. When will the men get penicillin?

BRODUS. *(Determined, not apologetic.)* When you're heading the foremost Negro hospital in white Alabama, you go along; you go a long, long way, to go along.

EVERS. Willie dreams of dancing in the Cotton Club. Don't seem fair to let him dream that dream.

BRODUS. He got any other dreams in his pocket?

EVERS. No.

BRODUS. Then I wouldn't rush to wake him up.

EVERS. *(After a moment.)* I get the feeling that I'm being taken up over the hill, Dr. Brodus.

BRODUS. How's that?

EVERS. That's when someone says, "See that hill right up there. You just got to walk to that hill." When you get to that hill, they say, "I didn't mean this one, I meant that one up there, farther along." So you go to that one. And then the next one and the next until you figure you've come so far, you might as well go the rest of the way. That's how you get taken up over the hill, Dr. Brodus. *(Willie is heard off-stage with Douglas.)* Willie's going to want some answers.

BRODUS. Yes he will.

EVERS. Dr. Brodus ... don't take him up over the hill.

BRODUS. Nurse Evers.

EVERS. Yes, sir.

BRODUS. You let me do the talking. *(Willie enters followed by Douglas. Willie sits, looking at Brodus.)*

WILLIE. Well?... Dr. Brodus? *(Brodus remains silent.)*

DOUGLAS. You've got bad blood, Willie.

WILLIE. *(Pause; Willie takes this in.)* Still? You been treating it for fourteen years.

DOUGLAS. Still.

WILLIE. And that's what's wrong with my gilleein'?

DOUGLAS. Yes.

WILLIE. What can you do about it?

DOUGLAS. There's not much we can do right now, Willie. I'm sorry.

EVERS. *(Interrupting.)* But we're working on something, Willie. We're working on it as hard and as fast as we can —

BRODUS. *(Gently, silencing her.)* Nurse Evers.

WILLIE.   You don't have anything?

DOUGLAS.   No.

WILLIE.   Nothing? Dr. Brodus?

BRODUS.   *(Pause.)* No.

WILLIE.   *(Frightened.)* Nurse Evers, you're here to stop that bad blood and so is Dr. Douglas and Dr. Brodus and the whole government. Right?

EVERS.   Yes.

WILLIE.   That's right, isn't it?

EVERS.   Yes, Willie, yes.

WILLIE.   And I'm doing the best I can on my gilleein'.

EVERS.   Yes.

WILLIE.   Now this bad blood?

EVERS.   Yes ... what's your question, Willie?

WILLIE.   My question is ... I don't mean nothing bad about you or anybody, Nurse Evers ... I'm just asking ...

EVERS.   Yes, Willie. You can ask. Don't worry. Go ahead. Ask.

WILLIE.   *(Frightened, a half-whisper, to Evers.)* Do I need new doctorin'? Do I need to go somewhere else and get me some different doctorin'? *(Covering his discomfort at having asked the question.)* I'm just asking, now, I'm just asking. I don't mean nothing bad by it. About you Dr. Brodus. Or Dr. Douglas. You neither. Nobody. I just don't want to die before I start winning again. *(Desperate.)* Used to be I'd look out and smile and it would all just happen. I ain't smilin' no more 'cause I'm lookin' down.

BRODUS.   Willie —

WILLIE.   You gotta be looking out at them people and smilin' and showin' off; showing you're easy; King Jackspring headin' for the Cotton Club.

BRODUS.   Willie, I want you to understand something.... I'm a doctor. And a research scientist. Research means finding new things to help people. That doesn't mean every single person is helped but it means that more people are helped than hurt. And all the people gain something. You understand, Willie?

WILLIE.   I understand my things. I understand horses. You understand science. If I need to know something about science, I come to you.

DOUGLAS. *(Breaking in.)* That's exactly right, Willie. And if I need advice about horses, I ask you. You know what decision to make for me because you understand all about horses. You're an expert. You know the right choice better than anyone when it comes to horses, don't you?

WILLIE. Yes, I do. You can bet on that.

DOUGLAS. *(Douglas looks at Brodus.)* I would bet on it, Willie. I certainly would. *(Douglas exits.)*

BRODUS. Willie?

WILLIE. Yes, Dr. Brodus?

BRODUS. *(Reconsidering what he was going to say.)* Thank you for coming to see me, Willie. *(Brodus exits.)*

EVERS. *(Pause; trying to change the mood.)* I got something for you. *(Evers takes out a hat, showing it to Willie.)* It's for you, Willie. It will help you win. *(She hands him the hat.)* You can't stop believing that you're going to win, Willie.

WILLIE. Do you believe it?

EVERS. *(Determined.)* Willie, I'm your nurse. Nurse Evers ain't leaving you with nothing. I never have. And I'm not now. I'm going to see you through this. You hear? Look at me now. You got to hope. And you got to believe that hope. That's the only way we survive. Now you wear that hat. And you win, you hear.

WILLIE. Yes, ma'am. *(Preoccupied; trying to believe it.)* Sure. "Over the top." That's what I got to keep thinking. *(As he exits, referring to the hat.)* Thank you for the kindness.

EVERS. *(Calling after him.)* You can't ever do a kindness too soon, Willie ... *(Turning and speaking to the audience, as testimony.)* That afternoon when Mr. Bryan, and Mr. Washington came round, I gave a hat to each. They thanked me and promised to wear them. And they did. But the big excitement that day was the United States Government certificate of appreciation given to each man for participating in the study for fourteen years. It had their name printed on it. In indelible ink. Mr. Washington especially liked that. And the government, Senator, gave each man fourteen dollars. A dollar a year. *(Lights crossfade. Evers crosses to Hodman.)*

Scene 4

1946. Outside the Possom Hollow Schoolhouse. Two weeks later. Evening. Hodman, carrying a long pine-bark log, comes forward to Evers. Willie, Ben, and Caleb remain standing in the shadows.

HODMAN.   Five nights, see. That's the thing. You gotta do it for five nights. Through the new moon.

EVERS.   And you think he'll feel better?

HODMAN.   Yes, ma'am. I know he will.

EVERS.   It won't hurt him, will it?

HODMAN.   Of course not. Helping not hurting that's my kind of business. I'll get him smiling again when he dances, you'll see. And he'll stop all that lookin' down.... You could use a little smiling medicine yourself.

EVERS.   Don't you be fussin' over me, now.

HODMAN.   *(Instructing her.)* Molasses and sulfur. Now that's a good spring tonic. I'll have some ready for you next time you visit. My wife uses it every month. Makes her less cranky when she's falling off the roof.

EVERS.   *(Laughing.)* You take that molasses and sulfur every month, Hodman, you'll be cranky too.

HODMAN.   That's it. That's the way. Got you showing your eye teeth behind a smile.... Now don't you worry, Nurse Evers. Good as new. You'll see ... *(Hodman crosses to Willie, Ben, and Caleb as they come forward. Lights crossfade to night, moonlight.)* You'll have to call me "doctor." "Dr. Hodman." *(Evers crosses U. and then stands witness, in the shadows of her memory. She is not part of the reality of the scene.)* Now call, Willie. High and clear. Like this. *(Demonstrates, creating a spell.)* Kaaaaaaaaaaaaaaaaaa. And look into the eyes of the moon.

WILLIE.   Seems spooky.

CALEB.   Useless, is what it is.

HODMAN.   *(Intent.)* It's going to heal you. But keep your feet on that bark. And roll up those pants. Get some moonlight on those legs. Now don't turn away. You got to keep facing the moon. Just like last night.

CALEB.   And the night before. And the night before that. And that night before that.

HODMAN.   It takes five nights, Caleb. I told you that. You gotta go right through the new moon.

CALEB.   What about ten nights, Hodman? What good that do?

HODMAN.   *(Stung.)* Caleb, don't you put that on me.

CALEB.   Who am I going to be putting it on?

HODMAN.   Your child weren't strong enough to take that medicine. If she had been, she wouldn't have passed. Now that's the truth.

CALEB.   No sir. No. Now don't you be putting it on my child. I'm not gonna let you do that. Your medicine weren't strong enough to heal my child. Now that's the truth.

HODMAN.   You dreamed of fire, Caleb. I can't be healing a child when her daddy's dreaming of trouble.

CALEB.   My child died choking on your medicine at midday. My dreaming had nothing to do with that.

BEN.   Hold on. Stop it, both you boys. You all forgetting who you're talking to.

CALEB.   *(Refusing to back down, he explodes.)* You all ain't thinking. You ain't thinking. What the doctor tell you, Willie? Doctor say you're sick. Right? *(Driven; to Ben.)* Say you're sick, Ben. Right? *(To Hodman.)* Say you're sick, Hodman. Right? *(Referring to himself.)* Say I'm sick. Right? *(Pleading.)* Now how in God's heaven are we going to get well unless we try something new. We gonna wait to heal ourselves when every which way you can see men in this county are lining up getting this new medicine and walking out free and easy. I talk to those men: "Where you going, Sam?" "I got bad blood. Gonna get me penicillin." "Where you going, Tom?" "I got bad blood. Gonna get me penicillin." That's all you hear all over this county. "I'm gonna get me penicillin. I'm gonna get me penicillin. I'm gonna get me penicillin." And what we do? We gonna "Kaaaaaaaaaaa" at the moon.

HODMAN.   All right. You choose, Willie. Caleb's medicine.

Or mine.

BEN.   Nurse Evers don't want us to get that medicine, Caleb.

CALEB.   So what. They all keeping us from that medicine. I don't care what Nurse Evers wants.

BEN.   Shut your mouth about her, Caleb. She stuck by us. She don't have to be driving us and doing what she doing for us and answering the prayers of every needy family in this county. Now you just shut your mouth about her. *(Pause; Hodman looks at Willie.)*

WILLIE.   Sorry, Caleb. *(Willie walks to Hodman and stands on the log.)*

HODMAN.   *(Hodman hands Willie a jar.)* Now drink some May tea, Willie. And let's roll up them pants some more.

BEN.   Hold on. Come here, Caleb. Come here. *(They move away.)* You a good man, Caleb. A strong man. You just don't see the world the way it is. You blind to a lot of things.

CALEB.   Like what things?

BEN.   Like Nurse Evers.... We talk ... she been asking after you. Think about it. Think about what you doing and who you doing it to when you say things like you said. *(Caleb does not reply; after a few moments he turns to leave.)* Where you going?

CALEB.   I'm going to think about what I'm doing, Ben. Just like you said. I gonna think. *(He exits.)*

HODMAN.   Drink that last swallow. That's it. Come on, Ben. We're wasting moonlight. Now, stand tall on this bark, Willie, and "call."

WILLIE.   Kaaaaa —

HODMAN.   More. Louder. Hit the moon. "Call" like your legs depended on it.

WILLIE.   *(Willie takes a deep breath and then makes a long, whistling, high-pitched, desperate call to the moon, a call filled with pain and rage.)* Kaaaaaaaaaaaaaaaaaaaaaaaaaaaaaaaaaaaaaaaa ... *(Lights crossfade. Brodus enters with Douglas following him. Evers crosses to them. Hodman and Ben exit. Willie moves to a dim backlight, isolated, intently practicing and testing his legs, intermittently resting.)*

DOUGLAS.   If you waver in the middle of this study no one

is going to trust you with future funding. Ever.

WILLIE. *(Dancing.)* One, two, over the top.

DOUGLAS. And what about your determination to prove equality of response to this disease?

BRODUS. It's been proven. Many times over.

DOUGLAS. No. Not if the data is incomplete.

BRODUS. Every time another patient, Negro or white, is cured with penicillin, it's proven again. The question is now irrelevant. There is no longer a need for this study.

DOUGLAS. The need is greater than ever.

BRODUS. Why?

DOUGLAS. Fear. *(Referring to data pages he is holding.)* The national will to eradicate any disease depends on continuing fear. Raw, personal fear in the right places. Only by parading the devastation caused to these patients can we guarantee a national fear fierce enough to stamp out this disease everywhere and completely and finally.... I want to treat them. But not yet. Not when the money for treating thousands might evaporate. And the Macon money would be the first to go.... You're fighting for 600 men. Try 6,000 men. Or 60,000. 600,000. That's our fight. *(Douglas exits.)*

WILLIE. *(Willie quietly resumes practicing.)* One, two, over the top.

EVERS. *(Over the end of Willie's line, confronting Brodus.)* Call him back here. Say something. Don't let him go.... Dr. Brodus, I know those numbers. They're my friends and neighbors. I sit beside those numbers in church. And I got news for you: You're one of those numbers, Dr. Brodus, and so am I. And so was yo' Mama and yo' Daddy. So if you come so far up, that you forget you Mama picking cotton, I'm reminding you now.... Damn. Damn you. *(Brodus does not acknowledge Evers. She has not in reality been speaking to him. Evers turns to the audience, as testimony.)* That's all of what I might have said right then. But all I said was, "I'm feeling deeply uneasy. I'm having more and more doubts." And I said all that to myself. *(Evers crosses to the schoolhouse as the lights crossfade and Brodus exits and Caleb enters.)*

Scene 5

1946. The interior of the Possom Hollow Schoolhouse. Three months later. Evening. Evers and Caleb stand looking at each other. For a brief moment nothing is said. Willie is still visible, now quietly resting his legs.

CALEB. Wasn't sure you'd show up.

EVERS. Me neither. You been all right?

CALEB. It's been four months.

EVERS. You're lucky.

CALEB. Maybe. *(Pause.)*

EVERS. I been worried about you, Caleb.

CALEB. Penicillin ain't bothering me. And moon calling ain't helping Willie.

EVERS. I know.

CALEB. You seen him?

EVERS. Yes.

CALEB. He needs penicillin, Nurse Evers. Give it to him.

EVERS. I can't do that.

CALEB. Why?

EVERS. *(Driving.)* I can't do it.

CALEB. How do you know you can't?

EVERS. I know from the United States government. That's how I know.

CALEB. Well, now you know from something else. From me. Right here. I got that penicillin. Look at me. Don't that tell you something. You tell that government, "no." ... And then you come along. With me.

EVERS. You leaving?

CALEB. For good. *(Pause.)* I'm asking you ... if ... if you want to come with me.

EVERS. Don't you understand me? At all?

CALEB. Sounds like you're telling me, I don't.

EVERS. Caleb, my calling is to serve my people. That's why I went to Tuskegee in the first place. To go out from there and do something for my people.

CALEB.   There's people everywhere.

EVERS.   Nowhere worse off than here. I got to see these home-people through whatever storms are blowing at them for as long as I'm walking and able.... Nursing is my life, Caleb, my oath, my calling.

CALEB.   I guess I got a calling too. To use my brain and my mouth instead of my hands and my back. That's what you told me, wasn't it? Fourteen years ago.

EVERS.   Fourteen years ago. Yes. That long.

CALEB.   *(Pause.)* Well? *(Pause; they look at each other. Evers does not approach him.)* Must be a comfort. To have an oath. You got a traveling oath for ordinary folk?

EVERS.   Be your brother's keeper and do what the Lord give you the strength to do. That's an ordinary oath. Good for one, good for all.

CALEB.   Well, I'll just keep that one in my pocket. *(Pause.)* "Eunice." Got nice in it, don't it?

EVERS.   I'll drive you.

CALEB.   No. Might as well start by myself. I got thirty miles by foot by morning. *(Evers watches Caleb exit. Lights crossfade.)*

WILLIE.   *(Suddenly.)* Hop, slide. *(He is dancing successfully but never free of the pain, quietly reciting his patter.)* Da, da, da, hop, slide. *(Evers notices the distant image of Willie and then is drawn to Ben as he enters in a wheelchair. Willie suddenly stops and starts rubbing his right knee with both hands. Lights fade to dim backlight on Willie and come up fully on Ben.)*

Scene 6

1946. Memorial hospital. Four months later. Ben sits in a wheelchair in a pool of light. Evers is instructing him. Willie sits waiting to regain enough strength to begin practicing again.

BEN.   Can't get no breath.

EVERS.   Hold your lips together. Like this. Breathe smooth and shallow.

BEN.   Kissin' lips?

EVERS.   That's right. *(Holding his hand, waiting a few moments.)* Better? That better?

BEN.   Better. Yes.

EVERS.   Good. *(Ben takes a breath or two until he feels comfortable.)*

BEN.   You know what I do most days now, Nurse Evers?

EVERS.   No. No I don't, Ben.

BEN.   Practice writing. My name. You gave me something when you started me on that writing.

EVERS.   That's good to hear.

BEN.   Seems like you been around forever.

EVERS.   That how I look?

BEN.   No. You look just like you did fourteen years ago at that Possom Hollow Schoolhouse.

EVERS.   You're blind.

BEN.   Not yet.... You seen my certificate?

EVERS.   You got it framed.

BEN.   It's the same size as my picture of President Roosevelt. I put a mirror in the middle. So I look at the President, and then at my award, and then myself. I look like a stranger to myself in that mirror. I can't sleep for wonderin' how sick I'll have to get before people won't be able to recognize me. *(He takes a breath.)* Wish my chest bones would grow bigger. Then I could feel like I have enough breath.

EVERS.   It's water, Ben. You're holding onto your water.

BEN.   You're sure you recognize me?

EVERS.   You look like Ben. Just like Ben. *(Pause.)* You got any relatives here?

BEN.   Don't got no relatives living here or anywhere near here.... What's bothering you?

EVERS.   Nothing. Got some business talk.

BEN.   All right.

EVERS.   You're the one to sign this paper, Ben. *(She shows him the paper.)*

BEN.   What's it say?

EVERS. (*Reading the paper for him.*) Says that you agree to the autopsy and that you get fifty dollars for your burying.
BEN.   What's an autopsy?
EVERS.   They take a look at you, Ben. After you're gone. To see what went wrong. They're gonna want to take a look at your heart.
BEN.   And my brain?
EVERS.   That too.
BEN.   No. I'm sorry. That don't fit my plans.
EVERS.   What plans?
BEN.   My funeral plans. Open casket and flowers and a wreath. Don't want to look like I been cut up in Mr. Tom's restaurant by the rough boys.
EVERS.   Ben, you're not going to look any different because of the autopsy.
BEN.   What about where they cut in to me. Into my chest and my head.
EVERS.   Ben —
BEN.   Yes —
EVERS.   They button you right up. It's all done in a way so you'll be laying back on the cuts and covered by a fine suit.
BEN.   What about my head? My face? How they going to look at my brain without messing up my face.... I want to look quiet and peaceful. I want to look like I'm resting.
EVERS.   You will.
BEN.   Serene and undisturbed?
EVERS.   Serene and peaceful.
BEN.   Don't know. This autopsy don't do me much good.
EVERS.   No.... But it's helping us learn and be a help to the others.... Ben, all these years ... you're part of something, something important, something lasting even after you pass on.
BEN.   I am?
EVERS.   Yes.
BEN.   "Miss Evers' Boys." ... Be nice to be part of something lasting longer than a season. (*Deciding.*) All right. That's a fair trade. (*Looking at the paper.*) Now I'm signing for real, huh? Something official. And with a pen ... (*He prints "BEN."*)

a main street with three dead ends, eh, Nurse Evers?

EVERS.   Yes.

BEN.   *(Struggles; finishes, proud.)* "Washington."

EVERS.   You did it.

BEN.   Yes, I did. I most certainly did. *(Evers collects the paper and looks at Ben.)*

EVERS.   Ben?

BEN.   Yes.

EVERS.   I'm sorry.

BEN.   For what?

EVERS.   For your trouble.

BEN.   Nurse Evers, but for you I'd been weighed down with a lot more than I had. My life could have been a lot better. And it could have been a lot worse.

EVERS.   Is that true?

BEN.   Yes, ma'am. You stood by us. You always treated us special. We always knew we'd be cared for, and that you'd be watching out for us. And my proudest time was those gillee contests and knowing that Nurse Evers was my nurse. Hey, you got nothing to be crying about. You didn't make me sick and you did all you could to make me well.... And I loved riding in that government car.

EVERS.   I'm a nurse, Ben. I follow what the doctors say.

BEN.   I know that. We all know. That's no crime. We're proud of you. Come on now. Stop that. Stop that crying. *(Ben sings "Oh, Children, Don't Be Afraid"* to comfort her. Then speaking.)* Here, hold old Ben's hand. Make you feel better. *(He sings. Evers joins in with him. She continues singing quietly under Ben's lines trying to comfort him.)* Nurse Evers, I know.

EVERS.   What you know, Ben?

BEN.   I know you'll do right by me. You always have.... There. I just got a deep, deep breath. Finally. That feel good. *(Ben closes his eyes to rest. He is holding Evers' hand. We hear Ben quietly humming "Children, Don't Be Afraid"* to himself as the*

---

* See Special Note on Songs and Recordings on copyright page.

lights crossfade and we see Willie *stand and prepare to dance again. Brodus and Douglas enter. Evers crosses to them but turns back to watch Ben during the first part of the following scene.)*

Scene 7

1946. Dr. Brodus' office. Two months later. Throughout the scene, Willie is quietly practicing and counting as he moves; at intervals he stops only to start again with renewed determination; he is not part of the scene in the office. During the first part of the scene, Evers hears Brodus and Douglas but continues to stare at Ben.

WILLIE. Over the top.
DOUGLAS. Penicillin won't help them. It's too late. The damage is done.
BRODUS. It would stop them from getting worse.... We're giving penicillin to every other syphilitic in the country regardless of how many years they've had the disease.
DOUGLAS. They're different.
BRODUS. How?
DOUGLAS. They're not in the study.
EVERS. *(As testimony.)* Mr. Benjamin Washington died at seventy-four years of age. *(Ben exits.)* A long life. But not a good one ... I got Mr. Washington that coffin. He looked serene and peaceful.
WILLIE. Over the top. *(Evers notices Willie and is then pulled back into the scene by Douglas' line.)*
DOUGLAS. *(Coming over the end of Willie's line.)* We cannot invalidate fourteen years work and the sacrifice of all those patients with a single injection that might be useless or lethal.
BRODUS. We have fourteen years of data.
DOUGLAS. *(Sharply.)* Fourteen years is not end point. It's scientifically incomplete if not taken to end point.
EVERS. End point?
DOUGLAS. If we're going to match the Oslo study, we

87

have no choice.... It's no longer our decision. It's Washington's decision. This study must go to end point.

EVERS.   And how far is that?

DOUGLAS.   Autopsy. The facts in this study must be validated by autopsy.

EVERS.   My patients shouldn't have to make that sacrifice.

DOUGLAS.   *(Losing his patience.)* They already have. Each year we get closer to unraveling the secrets of this disease because those few men have sacrificed for something greater than they'll ever understand. We owe it to those men to make this the best study possible.

EVERS.   I promised before God not to harm my patients. I promised before God to devote myself to the welfare of my patients.

DOUGLAS.   Nurse Evers ... I'd appreciate a follow-up call to every physician in the Tuskegee area. Make sure they understand that they're not to treat those men with penicillin. By mistake. *(Douglas exits.)*

WILLIE.   Gotta work, gotta work.

EVERS.   I've lied to those men because you told me to. I've misled them because I thought I could trust you with their welfare. Those men need penicillin. No one will help them if we don't. No one will help them if we don't.

BRODUS.   I understand your passion, Nurse Evers.

EVERS.   I'm not going up over that next hill, Dr. Brodus.

BRODUS.   *(Cutting her off, an explosion.)* You think you're the only person who feels? *(To Evers.)* You got your burden and I got mine. You serve the race in your way. I serve it in mine. I can't rock the boat while I'm trying to keep a people from drowning. There are trade-offs you can't even imagine. Don't you see that? *(In the background, Willie's practicing becomes more desperate.)* You spend your time around the colored. Good. Well, I spend mine tiptoeing around the white. But I ain't there to shine no shoes. And I ain't no Uncle Tom. And I ain't no shufflin' nigger. *(After regaining control, he looks at Evers.)* Is that colored enough for you, Nurse Evers? *(Brodus looks at Evers for a moment, turns and leaves. Willie is seen and heard simultaneous with Brodus' exit.)*

WILLIE. *(Reaching past the pain.)* Da, da, da, da, da.

EVERS. *(Lights change as Evers cries out through her own pain to both the exiting Brodus and to Hodman as he enters.)* We've got a choice right now.

Scene 8

1946. A field. Two days later. Evers confronts Hodman. Willie remains visible in the background, standing, still.

HODMAN. *(Continuing from the previous scene.)* What about?

EVERS. *(She takes out a vial of penicillin and shows it to Hodman.)* About this here new medicine that's been discovered.

HODMAN. Does it work?

EVERS. Yes, it works. You won't find any medicine better than this. I went to hell and back to get it for you.

HODMAN. Don't look like much. But I don't got nothing to lose.

EVERS. I got to tell you, there's a chance you might react bad to it.

HODMAN. Like kill me.

EVERS. I doubt it. I doubt it very much. But it's possible.

HODMAN. What they call it?

EVERS. Penicillin.

HODMAN. That's "Caleb's medicine." He keep yelling: "Get a hip shot of penicillin."

EVERS. Did you get it?

HODMAN. No. I don't figure I need Caleb's medicine when I got my own: You burn spider webs and look into the smoke. That's good for your eyesight, you know. But the webs are weak this year. Too wet.

EVERS. That what's bothering you? Your eyes?

HODMAN. Sometimes. I saw two door handles day before yesterday. But I'd been out in the sun.

EVERS. Hodman, I want you to take some of "Caleb's

medicine."

HODMAN.   I thought you didn't want us to take it.

EVERS.   You need it, Hodman. And you need it now.

HODMAN.   Why?

EVERS.   Those two door handles.

HODMAN.   Yeah.... That's what I been thinking.

EVERS.   *(As testimony.)* For three weeks I went out to Mr. Hodman Bryan's cotton field. I administered three million units of penicillin, every week. Right here. *(Referring to her hip.)* He kept screaming —

HODMAN.   Stop sticking me.

EVERS.   But I kept sticking. I was going to save that man. First Hodman Bryan. Then Willie Johnson. Then one by one. The others. That's how it was going to be.... On a Sunday evening, the fourth week, I found Mr. Bryan with a tin can and a rock crawling out between two rows of cotton. *(To Hodman.)* Hodman, what are you doing? *(Hodman is on his hands and knees rubbing the ground then killing red ants with a rock and then putting them in a 32-ounce can of turpentine. Throughout the following scene he brings a quiet clarity to his hallucinations. The nature of his disease is such that even in psychosis, he is calm and deliberate. This contrasts with Evers' growing anxiety and final emotional disintegration.)*

HODMAN.   Looking for red ants.

EVERS.   Why?

HODMAN.   To keep the ghosts away.

EVERS.   Hodman, look at me. Not there. Here. Hodman. In my eyes. Look at me,

HODMAN.   *(Calm.)* Can't. I'm looking for the baby. *(He continues rubbing the ground.)* There's buried money around haints, Nurse Evers. You help. I'll give you some. *(Suddenly seeing something.)* Nurse Evers, there she is. Caleb's baby. *(Hodman quickly walks in a wide circle.)* "Go devil, go devil, go devil."

EVERS.   *(To the audience.)* I followed him into the cotton field. There was a shattered oak at one end. That's where I found him. *(Hodman starts rubbing the ground again. Evers moves toward Hodman.)* Stop rubbing that ground and look at me.

90

What are you doing, Hodman?

HODMAN. *(With clarity.)* I'm making new medicine, Nurse Evers. I'm getting this mold to put in it. That's what penicillin is, ain't it? Mold?

EVERS. *(Cutting him off.)* Not that kind of mold.

HODMAN. I never got sick even when I was drinking, Nurse Evers. Now I'm eating the paint off the furniture. That's how I know I need my new medicine. *(He bangs on the can trying to open it.)*

EVERS. *(With growing alarm.)* Come on, Hodman. You got to go to the hospital.

HODMAN. Go devil. *(The hammering gets faster.)*

EVERS. Stop hammering at that can and come along with me. We're going to take a Chevy ride. *(Evers touches Hodman, trying to get his attention.)*

HODMAN. *(Recoiling from her touch.)* Tt, tt, tt, tt, tt, tt. *(He opens the can, a triumphant shout.)* There. *(With clarity.)* Now you put the mold in, Nurse Evers. And then you mix it. Like this, see. Smooth. *(He does so.)* Now the words. *(He finds the direction of the moon and says once, deeply, as an incantation.)*
"Blue Night Blue,
New Moon White,
Night Owl Cries,
Clear My Eyes."
(He suddenly holds up the "medicine" and calls to the moon.)
Kaaaaaaaaaaaaaaaaaaaaaaaaaaaaaaa ... *(Evers realizes Hodman is going to drink poison. She tries to pull the can from his hands; he protects his "medicine" by pulling it away from her. The following dialogue is meant to convey Evers' emotional response to Hodman and to the Senator who is asking her about Hodman. In this section Evers is present in both plays — the chronological play and the testimony play — at once. She remains in the action with Hodman even when she speaks the line addressed to the Senator. The scene's focus should be on Evers' emotional disintegration, a disintegration that is accelerated by Evers' growing certainty that she is an accomplice in Hodman's madness.)*

EVERS. Give that to me.

HODMAN. No. *(Reasonably.)* Can't. This here skull and cross-

91

bones on the can means it's private food.

EVERS.   Put that down. That's poison.

HODMAN.   Poison. No. Penicillin. *(Hodman calls with increased force.)* Kaaaaaaaaaaa ... *(Willie, U., joins in this "call," a combination of a bird sound and a baby cry. Willie's reality is separate from Hodman and Evers and his presence is not acknowledged.)*

WILLIE.   *(A single call.)* Kaaaaaaaaaaaaaaaaaaaaaaaa.... *(Willie kneels holding his leg.)*

EVERS.   *(Evers struggles with Hodman.)* That's not medicine. I told him it wasn't medicine, Senator. Put it down. Hodman. I told him. I yelled and yelled and yelled. *(Suddenly, Evers desperately fights for the can, screaming as her terror increases.)* That's poison. It will kill you. You hear me? Don't drink it. Please. Listen to me now. Hodman. Please, Hodman. *(Evers struggles with Hodman.)* I tried to make him look at me, Senator. I tried to make him hear me.

HODMAN.   *(Overlapping.)* Get away, you.

EVERS.   *(Simultaneous with Hodman's call and Willie's cry.)* NO. Hodman. NO. NO. Don't drink it. NO, Hodman, don't drink it. NO ...

HODMAN/WILLIE.   *(Simultaneous.)* Kaaaaaaaaaaaaaaaaaaaaaaaa ...

EVERS.   *(As Hodman throws Evers to the ground and takes a long swallow, Evers screams.)* NOOOO ... *(Light out on Willie; he exits. After a while, broken.)* No, Senator, no.

HODMAN.   *(Hodman finishes the liquid and then stands; calmly.)* There. *(He looks around.)* That baby's gone, Nurse Evers. *(As he exits apparently cured.)* That haint done skipped on home. *(Evers recovers and stands to give testimony.)*

EVERS.   *(As testimony.)* Mr. Hodman Bryan died of convulsions caused by the ingestion of thirty-two ounces of turpentine. A footnote in the autopsy report mentioned "elements curiously consistent with those found in the Herxheimer reaction to penicillin." I never found out for sure. Who could I ask, Senator? *(It is difficult for her to continue.)* I HAD KILLED THAT MAN.... After that, Senator, I just fell in line. *(Lights crossfade as scene changes to the Epilogue.)*

Epilogue

1972. Outside the Possom Hollow Schoolhouse. A crisp American flag and a printed sign are tacked to the decaying wood. The sign reads: "United States Senate Testimony Site; Location: (written in by hand.) Possom Hollow School; Date: (written in by hand.) April 24, 1972." Brodus and Douglas are sitting waiting to testify.

EVERS.   *(As testimony.)* Those that got out were safe. Mr. Willie Johnson left Macon county for Tipton County, Tennessee, in 1956. He got that hip shot of penicillin in Tipton and that's why he can use a cane now instead of crutches. Mr. Caleb Humphries got out too. He became a preaching man, with a traveling circuit. I lost track of them after they left Macon…. We used to tell the men that this disease had three parts: you get it, you forget it and then you regret it twenty or thirty years later when it comes back to haunt you. That's how it's been with me too. I tried to stop thinking about it after 1946. The men were set apart from the thousands that were treated with penicillin and the study continued. "The Tuskegee Study of Untreated Syphilis in the Negro Male" had acquired a life of its own. It had become … familiar. Each spring I prepared a report on the number of patients remaining: four hundred and twelve in 1946; three hundred and sixty ten years later; one hundred and twenty-seven this year, 1972. *(Evers sits. Caleb enters from the schoolhouse on his way to get Willie. Caleb sees Douglas and stops.)*
CALEB.   You into pork, Dr. Douglas?
DOUGLAS.   That statement was taken out of context.
CALEB.   And a very down-home way of puttin' it: "A great hog has been made out of a very small pig."
DOUGLAS.   I was commenting on a statement by the mayor of Tuskegee; the original statement was not mine.
CALEB.   But very down-home it was, nonetheless. And you agreed with it. From listening to your testimony inside, I

93

mean. And as soon as I heard what you said I knew I had to ask you one question.

DOUGLAS.   All right, what question?

CALEB.   You got any more pigs cookin'? 'Cause if you do I hope you learned the difference between treatin' and watchin'.

DOUGLAS.   Mr. Humphries —

CALEB.   Reverend Humphries.

DOUGLAS.   Reverend Humphries, those were not racial decisions: those were research options that were appropriate at the time.

CALEB.   *(Stopping him.)* Don't get me wrong, Dr. Douglas. I don't think it was forty years of "garbage science" or whatever the newspapers are calling it. Because I got something useful out of all this.

DOUGLAS.   You did?

CALEB.   Fourteen dollars. And that certificate of participation for being a good patient for fourteen years. *(He takes out the certificate.)*

DOUGLAS.   That seems pretty useless to me.

CALEB.   Well, that's what I thought. But I searched for that certificate for two days when all this blew up. I said to myself, Dr. Douglas, I said: "I gotta find that certificate. I gotta find it and give it to my lawyer." *(Caleb exits. Evers, Brodus, and Douglas sit in silence.)*

EVERS.   *(To Dr. Brodus.)* What will they do to you?

BRODUS.   Nothing. At my age I've got nothing to lose. *(Ironic.)* Except my good name. *(They wait.)*

DOUGLAS.   That data has been used and will be used again and every time it is used that researcher is saying I believe in that study. *(Pause; no one speaks.)* Dr. Brodus, that data proved that black and white are affected in exactly the same way. That's what you wanted to prove, wasn't it? Those statistics helped you stand up against racial bias.

BRODUS.   *(Eye to eye.)* Those men could have been given a choice.

DOUGLAS.   Those men were serving their race. *(Silence. Douglas, Evers and Brodus sit and wait. Caleb enters with Willie who is using a cane. Caleb is carrying the Victrola and walking with Willie toward the schoolhouse where Willie will testify. Willie's walk must not be exaggerated. It consists of a slight limp and weakness in one leg. He uses his cane to compensate for this disability. He walks slowly but with dignity. Evers hears the following dialogue.)*

CALEB. *(To Willie.)* That's what that newspaper article was saying, Willie. That's what "guinea pig" means. They were all just watching us to see what the bad blood would do.

WILLIE. Nurse Evers?

CALEB. She took you out of that Birmingham line, didn't she? That penicillin could have saved Ben and Hodman and made you a dancin' man.

WILLIE. *(He is still uncertain.)* Nurse Evers?

CALEB. Nurse Evers, and that man there and that man. And all those doctors from Washington. Watchin' and waitin'. Waitin' for us to die. *(Guiding him toward the schoolhouse.)* Come on.

WILLIE. *(Pause; refusing to accept completely what Caleb is saying, he looks at Evers and moves toward her. To Evers.)* Nurse Evers.... You was a friend to me.

EVERS. I am a friend to you, Willie.

WILLIE. What kind of friend could do what you did?

EVERS. Understand, Willie. You have to try to understand.

WILLIE. You try to understand me. That penicillin would have made it so I could walk without pain and maybe even Jackspring. And they didn't give that to me in Birmingham because you pulled me out of that line so I could be a part of Miss Evers' Boys and Burial Society. So you all could do your watching while I wake up past midnight not feeling my legs or else feeling pain, burning pain like a hot iron pressin' on my skin, 'til I shout, "Take this pain away. Lord, please, take this pain away." My body was my freedom. You hear me? MY BODY WAS MY FREEDOM. *(He takes the Victrola from Caleb and puts it down.)* You all wanna watch. Watch now. Watch and think what I used to do with my feet and what I could have done; how my feet sounded faster than this here music could have pushed them. You all want to watch? Watch. *(With difficulty Willie starts the music. Caleb remembers the*

95

music. The two men enjoy the remembrance for a moment.) "Drop over, double step; drop over, double step; drop over step, step, strut." Lord, you remember that, Caleb? *(They laugh; but as Willie listens to the music, and as he remembers the way he used to be able to dance, his rage increases. This memory becomes more vivid as he turns to Evers and recites the patter he used to say.)* "Drop over, double step"? *(Standing still, sharply, to the others.)* You watchin'? "Gillee strut, down, drop; gillee strut down, drop, drop." Watch. You watch this now. *(Spurred by his own anger, he forces himself to tap his cane and slightly shuffle one foot, a broken suggestion of his former skill. He can do no more and refuses to humiliate himself by trying. He stands with dignity and recites.)* "Gillee, drop, drop, drop, drop, down, drop, down, drop, down ..." Watch. *(Willie stops tapping his cane and foot. Keeping an eye on them, he uses the patter to make them watch his stillness.)* "Drop, down, drop, drop, drop, down; *(A shout of anguish; he doesn't move.)* WATCH, and remember: drop, down, down, down, down ..." *(Willie gives up the memory and hits the Victrola with his cane, stopping it. Silence. Willie stands perfectly still. Evers moves to comfort Willie.)* NO. NO HELP. *(Willie moves away; to Evers, tapping his cane.)* ... I can walk pretty good on this stick. *(Willie exits into the schoolhouse. Caleb follows him. Douglas exits. Brodus exits. After Willie is gone, Caleb returns to retrieve the Victrola. Evers sits and avoids his glance. Caleb begins to exit toward the schoolhouse.)*

EVERS.   *(Suddenly.)* I LOVED YOU MEN. I looked after you as if you were my own. I got you free care and doctorin' that no one could afford back then.

CALEB.   And you got us buried.

EVERS.   Yes, that too. You're too far away now to recall what a decent burial meant in those days. You're just one step, too far away.

CALEB.   And if I hadn't taken that step, I'd never have gotten penicillin.

EVERS.   Those men had some peace and some suffering. Whose to say they wouldn't have had the suffering without the peace if I hadn't come along.

CALEB.   *(Trying to understand.)* What made you do it?...

What made you do it?

EVERS. NURSING WAS MY LIFE, Caleb. You know that. Those ideals have guided my life.

CALEB. What ideals?

EVERS. Treat every patient the same. Follow what the doctors say.

CALEB. *(Looking at her.)* Eunice Evers ... Eunice Evers, you did those ideals proud. *(He exits; Evers waits; we hear Caleb's car start and drive away. Evers comes forward; all lights dim except for a spotlight on Evers.)*

EVERS. In the testimony today, there was a man gracious enough to wonder what effect the scandal, as he put it, might have on the public health nurse who had worked with the participants and who lived in Tuskegee. "She has been known throughout the program as a selfless woman," he said, "who devoted her entire career to this project." And then he was kind enough to hope that it would "not be necessary for her to share any of the blame."

Well, now there's big blame and then there's little blame. The big blame — that seems to be going to the government and those doctors.

Some people in Macon are even saying the government gave those men that disease in the first place. I can't let myself be thinking about that. I got enough thinking to do just handling the little blames.

Those are the blames that got nothing to do with talk about right and wrong and black and white and guinea pigs and money. Those little blames are when you go back to where you live, lived for your whole life, and catch your friends looking at you for no seeming reason, and people walk by you and don't say "good morning" and they don't use your name when they're giving you change as if using it would dirty their mouths up some. Newspapers don't publish stories about these little blames but they mount up and they're strong and they push you to live a new way of life. *(Strong, not apologetic or self-pitying.)* I loved those men. Those men were susceptible to kindness. *(A snare drum is heard. In the shadows Ben and Hodman and Caleb appear in white tux and*

97

tails dressed as they might have appeared if they had ever made it to the Cotton Club. Miss Evers' Boys are a silent, antique still photograph. Willie re-enters to the fragile rustling of the snare drum. Willie, also dressed for the Cotton Club, dances smoothly between the shadows of the other characters, a dry leaf scattering brilliant turns and twists into the wind. Evers looks then turns away facing the audience. The drum fades to silence. Willie's graceful, haunting dance continues.)

WILLIE.   *(Whispered.)* Da, da, da, da, daaaaaaa. *(Lights fade.)*

END OF PLAY

PROPERTY LIST

American flag
Printed sign: "United States Senate Testimony Site;
                 Location: Possum Hollow School
                 Date: April 24, 1972"
Instruments:
         Heavy metal oil drum with sling (HODMAN)
         Washtub bass with kazoo and bells (BEN)
         Tin can megaphone with harmonica (CALEB)
Schoolbell rope (CALEB)
Blackboard (WILLIE, CALEB, DR. BRODUS, DR. DOUGLAS)
Chalk (WILLIE, CALEB, DR. BRODUS, DR. DOUGLAS)
Mole's foot necklace (HODMAN)
Paper, pens (EVERS)
Doctor's bag, new (DR. DOUGLAS)
Clipboard (DR. DOUGLAS)
Surgical instruments (EVERS)
Tourniquet (DR. DOUGLAS)
Needle (DR. DOUGLAS)
Victrola (HODMAN)
Mercury salve in a large, white jar (EVERS)
Poster advertising free treatment of syphilis
White hospital gowns (EVERS, CALEB, DR. DOUGLAS)
Face masks (EVERS, DOUGLAS)
Antiseptic solution (EVERS)
Surgical gloves (DR. DOUGLAS)
Spinal tap needle (DR. DOUGLAS)
Test tube (DR. DOUGLAS)
Fluid (DR. DOUGLAS)
Small wooden staircase (BEN)
Suitcase (WILLIE)
Seal of the United States Public Health Service
Banner with: MISS EVERS' BOYS
2 microscopes, with slides
2 benches (CALEB, WILLIE, EVERS)
Hat (EVERS)

Pine-bark log (HODMAN)
Pages with data (DR. DOUGLAS)
Wheelchair (BEN)
Paper to sign (EVERS)
Pen (BEN)
Rock (HODMAN)
32-oz. can of turpentine (HODMAN)
Certificate (CALEB)
Cane (WILLIE)

SOUND EFFECTS

Gilee music
Train whistle
Car honk
Car starting
Snare drum

NEW PLAYS

★ **RABBIT HOLE by David Lindsay-Abaire.** Winner of the 2007 Pulitzer Prize. Becca and Howie Corbett have everything a couple could want until a life-shattering accident turns their world upside down. "An intensely emotional examination of grief, laced with wit." *–Variety.* "A transcendent and deeply affecting new play." *–Entertainment Weekly.* "Painstakingly beautiful." *–BackStage.* [2M, 3W] ISBN: 978-0-8222-2154-8

★ **DOUBT, A Parable by John Patrick Shanley.** Winner of the 2005 Pulitzer Prize and Tony Award. Sister Aloysius, a Bronx school principal, takes matters into her own hands when she suspects the young Father Flynn of improper relations with one of the male students. "All the elements come invigoratingly together like clockwork." *–Variety.* "Passionate, exquisite, important, engrossing." *–NY Newsday.* [1M, 3W] ISBN: 978-0-8222-2219-4

★ **THE PILLOWMAN by Martin McDonagh.** In an unnamed totalitarian state, an author of horrific children's stories discovers that someone has been making his stories come true. "A blindingly bright black comedy." *–NY Times.* "McDonagh's least forgiving, bravest play." *–Variety.* "Thoroughly startling and genuinely intimidating." *–Chicago Tribune.* [4M, 5 bit parts (2M, 1W, 1 boy, 1 girl)] ISBN: 978-0-8222-2100-5

★ **GREY GARDENS book by Doug Wright, music by Scott Frankel, lyrics by Michael Korie.** The hilarious and heartbreaking story of Big Edie and Little Edie Bouvier Beale, the eccentric aunt and cousin of Jacqueline Kennedy Onassis, once bright names on the social register who became East Hampton's most notorious recluses. "An experience no passionate theatergoer should miss." *–NY Times.* "A unique and unmissable musical." *–Rolling Stone.* [4M, 3W, 2 girls] ISBN: 978-0-8222-2181-4

★ **THE LITTLE DOG LAUGHED by Douglas Carter Beane.** Mitchell Green could make it big as the hot new leading man in Hollywood if Diane, his agent, could just keep him in the closet. "Devastatingly funny." *–NY Times.* "An out-and-out delight." *–NY Daily News.* "Full of wit and wisdom." *–NY Post.* [2M, 2W] ISBN: 978-0-8222-2226-2

★ **SHINING CITY by Conor McPherson.** A guilt-ridden man reaches out to a therapist after seeing the ghost of his recently deceased wife. "Haunting, inspired and glorious." *–NY Times.* "Simply breathtaking and astonishing." *–Time Out.* "A thoughtful, artful, absorbing new drama." *–Star-Ledger.* [3M, 1W] ISBN: 978-0-8222-2187-6

DRAMATISTS PLAY SERVICE, INC.
440 Park Avenue South, New York, NY 10016 212-683-8960 Fax 212-213-1539
postmaster@dramatists.com www.dramatists.com